Birthright funds medical research for the better health of women and their babies in hospitals and universities all over Britain. Gynaecological conditions such as menopause, infertility and women's cancer are included in Birthright's research brief but the charity is better known for its work with pregnancy and childbirth and in particular the problems of babies before, during and immediately after birth.

Birthright is the appeal arm of the Royal College of Obstetricians and Gynaecologists. H.R.H. The Princess of Wales has been Patron of Birthright since 1984.

Penny Junor is a writer, journalist and presenter of Channel 4's 4 *What It's Worth*.

Birthright

RESEARCH FOR HEALTHIER BABIES & HEALTHIER WOMEN

WHAT EVERY WOMAN NEEDS TO KNOW

Facts and Fears about Pregnancy, Childbirth and Womanhood

Foreword by H.R.H. The Princess of Wales

Edited by Penny Junor

CENTURY

London Melbourne Auckland Johannesburg

First published in 1988 by Century Hutchinson Ltd
Brookmount House, 62–65 Chandos Place,
London WC2N 4NW

Century Hutchinson Australia (Pty) Ltd
PO Box 496, 16–22 Church Street, Hawthorn,
Victoria 3122, Australia

Century Hutchinson New Zealand Ltd
PO Box 40–086, 32–34 View Road, Glenfield,
Auckland 10, New Zealand

Century Hutchinson South Africa (Pty) Ltd
PO Box 337, Bergvlei, 2012 South Africa

Photoset by Deltatype Ltd, Ellesmere Port
Printed and bound in Great Britain by
Anchor Brendon Ltd, Tiptree, Essex

Reprinted 1988 (twice)

British Library Cataloguing in Publication Data

Junor, Penny
    What every woman needs to know: facts
    and fears about pregnancy, childbirth
    and womanhood.
    1. Pregnancy   2. Childbirth
    I. Title
    618.2   RG524

ISBN 0–7126–1623–3

Contents

KENSINGTON PALACE

Since I became Patron of Birthright in 1984, I have met a number of women who have had healthy babies thanks to the research work of the charity. However, many people are still unaware that the research undertaken by Birthright covers not only pregnancy, but also many gynaecological problems, from cancer to infertility.

Each year Birthright receives enquiries from women who want to know whether new research will be of benefit to them and how to seek more information about their particular problem. This book is for these women. It is written by acknowledged experts in the clearest possible language and outlines the causes and treatments of those areas of difficulty most commonly encountered.

I am delighted that a book which will be beneficial to so many women will also help to ensure Birthright's future research.

Diana.

Introduction

Birthright is the appeal arm of the Royal College of Obstetricians and Gynaecologists. I became a member of the Royal College and started practising obstetrics in 1954. If such a book as this had been prepared then, the list of chapters would have been very different. Rhesus babies were a cause of grave concern then, but now, with the use of anti-D injections, rhesus babies are largely a problem of the past. In 1954, the use of obstetric ultrasound was still a gleam in the eye of its inventor, Professor Ian Donald. Today ultrasound has revolutionised the practice of obstetrics. Many of the drugs now used to alleviate infertility were not available on a widespread basis; but then neither was the contraceptive pill whose use is now taken for granted.

Research has made all these advances possible and has thereby ensured better health for many more women and their babies. But whilst the above are dramatic examples of what can be done, many women wonder, particularly when they encounter a common problem themselves, whether research is able to help them. Each chapter of this book therefore, outlines a specific problem and relates the advances that have been made and the treatments now available in a commendably clear and understandable way.

This book should change its function dramatically. For it should become a history book and let us hope, given the continued existence of Birthright, that it becomes a work of history sooner rather than later.

George Pinker
President
Royal College of Obstetricians and Gynaecologists

Acknowledgements

I would like to express sincere thanks to the contributors of this book who all donated their chapters and who have been so generous with their time and expertise – and patient with me. Without them there would obviously have been no book; but there have been others too, whose names do not appear in the text, yet whose help has been invaluable and who deserve special mention. Professor Geoffrey Chamberlain who has acted as medical advisor is one of them. His contribution has been enormous and I am very grateful to him. Huge thanks also to Jean Corroll for everything she has done – tasks too numerous to list. Finally my debt to Vivienne Parry, National Organiser of Birthright, who has been a joy to work with. Without her, and her unshakable sense of humour, none of this would have been possible.

Penny Junor   February 1988

About Birthright and its Research

Birthright funds medical research for the better health of women and their babies in hospitals and universities all over Britain. Gynaecological conditions such as menopause, infertility and women's cancer are included in Birthright's research brief but the charity is better known for its work with pregnancy and childbirth and in particular the problems of babies before, during and immediately after birth.

Birthright is the appeal arm of the Royal College of Obstetricians and Gynaecologists. H.R.H. The Princess of Wales has been Patron of Birthright since 1984.

Birthright funds research in two ways; research projects are supported for one, two or occasionally three years. Each project costs up to £50,000 in total and has a specific objective. About twenty new projects are funded each year and these projects are chosen, after rigorous scientific assessment by our research panel and external referees, from a field of one hundred or more applications submitted to us annually. Birthright grant holders are not necessarily doctors – they can be technicians, midwives or scientists – anyone in fact with a good idea which Birthright feels might be of practical benefit to women and their babies.

Birthright also funds five research centres. These receive more substantial funding (up to £500,000) over a five year period. Not only is research undertaken into a specific area of difficulty, but the unit serves as a centre for the treatment of patients and the training of doctors. Five areas are currently covered; the high risk fetus (King's College Hospital, London), unexplained infertility (Jessop Hospital, Sheffield), recurrent miscarriage (St Mary's Hospital, Paddington), high blood pressure in pregnancy (John Radcliffe Hospital, Oxford) and cervical cancer (University of Aberdeen).

Almost all of the topics covered by the chapters in this book have been the subject of Birthright research. Some, as can be seen from the work of our Centres, are the subject of intensive investigation by us. It is very likely that a problem that you have encountered is, or has been, covered by Birthright – so please ask us if you want to know about a particular area of research.

In the final analysis, Birthright is about good health and good news. If you feel that you have benefited from our research, why not help us to ensure that someone else can also benefit from our work in the future. Get in touch with us and we will tell you how to help us.

Vivienne Parry
National Organiser

Birthright
27 Sussex Place
Regent's Park
London
NW1 4SP   01 723 9296

1
Nutrition in Pregnancy

Frank Hytten

The most important aspect of nutrition in relation to pregnancy is that you are in good condition at the time of conception. Women who have been well fed all their lives and who are well grown and healthy have few problems with child-bearing. Whatever the mother eats during her pregnancy you can be sure that the fetus will be extremely well protected against even major vagaries of its mother's diet.

In this chapter we look at some of the normal changes that take place in the digestive tract which may cause symptoms and anxiety; and the more important aspects of diet in pregnancy.

Changes in the Digestive Tract

The digestive tract, in common with the rest of the body, undergoes profound and widespread changes during normal pregnancies and some of these may cause symptoms which could worry you.

It is usual in pregnancy for the gums to become swollen and spongy. Although this is not harmful, it does mean that they are more fragile and may bleed easily with tooth brushing. Do keep brushing, however, as you will be more liable to infection round the gums which may encourage dental caries. So thorough cleaning with a soft brush is important. The teeth themselves are not otherwise liable to decay because of the pregnancy.

The oesophagus or gullet is the source of the common and distressing symptom of heartburn, a purely mechanical problem where the closure between the gullet and the stomach becomes inefficient and allows stomach acid to move back towards the mouth. It is therefore often worse when circumstances assist that back flow – for example, lying flat or bending over so that the stomach is compressed by the uterus. Heartburn at night is often helped by raising the head of the bed a little. Avoid big meals which distend the stomach, particularly before going to bed. Sometimes you can work out which particular foods or drinks provoke heartburn and avoid them. Antacids are often helpful, but consult your doctor if you find yourself taking a lot of them.

The stomach becomes very sluggish in pregnancy and meals remain within it for much longer than usual. This normally causes no symptoms, except for making you more liable to nausea, particularly in early pregnancy and after sugary drinks. The phenomenon is otherwise unimportant, but if you take regular medication with tablets they may be absorbed more slowly and more irregularly than usual and you should ask your doctor about this.

As stomach secretions, including acid, are reduced during pregnancy, peptic ulceration is rare and women who already have ulcers usually have their symptoms relieved.

As well as the stomach, the whole bowel behaves sluggishly. That in itself has no ill effect and you may not be aware of it except if you find constipation a problem. The best way to cope with this is by increasing the bulk of your diet with wholemeal bread and vegetables, but if you feel some medication is necessary only use the mildest of laxatives.

Diet in Pregnancy

Some of the specific nutritional needs of pregnancy are in-escapable. Much of the new tissue which you will accumulate is an important and inherent part of every healthy pregnancy: the fetus itself and its placenta, the enlarged uterus, the increased breast tissue and a large expansion of the blood. All those extra tissues represent the storage of about 2 lb (nearly 1 kg) of protein. In addition, the average healthy mother puts on about 8 or 9 lb (about 4 kg) of body fat in the first two-thirds of pregnancy, mostly around the hips and trunk. This provides a big energy reserve for late pregnancy when the fetus is growing fast, and later for milk production. Although this makes sense in evolutionary terms, it is probably not essential, and in general there seems to be no obvious penalty for those women who do not put on this temporary fat store.

The ideal weight gain in pregnancy from almost every point of view is 24 to 28 lb (10 to 12 kg), about 1 lb (0.45 kg) per week after early pregnancy, and that allows for the accumulation of all the essential tissues, the growth of a good-sized baby and a temporary maternal deposit of fat.

The body also needs to provide energy for the extra 'work' it has to do to support the pregnancy: for such additional activities as the metabolism of the fetus and the other new tissues, and the increased work of breathing, of heart action and of the kidneys.

The total cost of all these components is about 70,000 to 80,000 calories, about two-thirds of which is 'capital gains' – the growth of new tissue; the rest is 'running costs'. That averages out at about 400 calories per day for the last two-thirds of pregnancy, a very uniform addition which is mostly 'capital gains' at the beginning when fat is being laid down, and mostly 'running costs' at the end when the fetus is large and using a lot of energy.

In fact, the average pregnant woman in Britain eats no more than an extra 200 calories per day above her ordinary intake, not 400, and the difference is due to the fact that while she still cannot escape the expenditure of that extra 200 calories for the specific needs of pregnancy she can economise by doing less of the things she ordinarily does. It is not just that she rests more and spends more time in bed – that may be difficult if she has other young children – but the ordinary activities of life are performed more economically. She is more relaxed when she does sit down, fidgets less, and makes a minimum of unnecessary movements.

Appetite and food preference
Appetite increases in early pregnancy and although some women don't notice that they are eating more, many experience a real surge of appetite. There is an even more conspicuous increase in thirst. In general, if left to herself, the pregnant woman will just eat more of her ordinary diet. Taste is altered, however, so that there may be a strong preference for certain foods and a dislike, even aversion, for others, particularly tea and coffee. Most women find themselves wanting salty and strongly flavoured foods and go off sweet things, but the reverse may also occur with occasional cravings for such things as fruit or chocolate. The change in taste may occasionally extend to pica – the desire to eat substances normally regarded as inedible, such as coal, soap or toothpaste. None of these changes of taste, however bizarre they may seem, are harmful.

Your diet and the baby's well-being
The fetus is equipped through its placenta to take from the

mother anything it needs, even at the expense of the mother's health. For the ordinarily well-nourished woman her fetus has no problem. If the mother eats the extra food which is needed to gain 1 lb of weight per week, not only will her own and her baby's energy needs be fully satisfied, but there will be ample protein and other nutrients for a healthy baby since a reasonable diet will contain all the necessary protein, vitamins and minerals in relation to the extra calories. There is no need to drink large amounts of milk, for example, to supply the baby with calcium; even if you drink none at all there are huge reserves of calcium in your own bones which can readily supply the small needs of the fetus.

We have good reason to be confident about this because an extreme example has been studied. During the very severe winter of 1944–5 a wartime blockade caused famine in north-west Holland, with average energy intakes of well under 1,000 calories per day. Women who were pregnant during the six months of extreme deprivation had babies who were well grown but very thin, with an average birthweight about a pound below normal. These babies were apparently unaffected by the experience: at the age of eighteen they were of normal height and their intellectual ability was unimpaired.

A more debatable question is whether the baby may sometimes be at risk from lack of trace minerals and vitamins. Iron and folic acid are discussed below in relation to the mother's own health; but even if the mother is marginally deficient the baby sees to its own supplies and quite severe iron deficiency in the mother does not lead to iron deficiency in the baby at birth.

More recently it has been suggested that pregnant women should take supplements of zinc on the grounds that marginal deficiency may affect the baby. There is no convincing evidence for this and you must be careful about taking zinc (or indeed any other supplement) without expert advice because the side effects may be more dangerous than any likely deficiency.

In that context there has been a great deal of recent debate about the value of taking multivitamin supplements before pregnancy to protect the baby against possible congenital defects. Again the evidence is far from clear and there is even concern that it could be harmful to take large amounts of vitamins. The Medical Research Council has launched an enquiry into the possible value of pre-pregnancy supplementation and we should await their verdict.

Finally alcohol and caffeine. There is no doubt that alcohol abuse will damage the fetus, but whether 'social drinking' can do so is not known. Present evidence suggests that moderate drinking – two alcoholic drinks per day – will not harm the fetus, but until we can be more certain the less alcohol you drink the better. The effect of caffeine from beverages such as tea, coffee and some proprietary soft drinks has been examined closely, but there is no evidence it causes harm. At least one official body, however, recommends that you should take such drinks sparingly.

Your diet and your own well-being
As we have seen, the fetus has powerful safeguards against dietary inadequacies in its mother, but pregnancy leads to nutritional stresses on the woman, some of them imposed not so much by nature but by her medical advisers.

Should weight gain be restricted? The practice is now much less common. For many years obstetricians have sought to impose an upper limit on the weight gained by pregnant women. They did so, and still do, for two main reasons: one, to reduce the likelihood of the mother developing the common and potentially serious complication of pre-eclampsia (see chapter 7); the other was to prevent the storage of fat which, because it is no longer needed in Western society as a safeguard, might in successive pregnancies lead stepwise into middle-aged obesity. Neither can be justified. There is undoubtedly an association between the amount of weight gained in pregnancy and the incidence of pre-eclampsia. That is to say women who develop the condition tend to have gained more weight than those who do not; but the excess weight of pre-eclampsia is mostly water, which will be unaffected by diet, and the fact is that restricting the weight gain by diet does not influence the incidence, or delay the onset, of pre-eclampsia.

If restricting weight gain does nothing for pre-eclampsia, does it help the mother regain her figure? Is the fat stored around the hips merely a redundant evolutionary hangover? The answer is no. The fat is stored under the influence of a pregnancy hormone and when that hormone level subsides so does the fat. Women tend to become heavier with age, but bearing two or three children has been shown to add an average of no more than about 2 lb by middle age. An extensive study of women who were identical twins, where only one of the pair had borne children, came to a similar conclusion.

There is another side to the weight gain coin. Women who gain much less weight than average tend to have small babies. Again the association does not lend itself to dietary manipulation. Many women, by no means all, who are gaining relatively little weight do so *because* the pregnancy is not going well and the baby is not growing. Making the mother eat more food will not make the baby grow any better.

Finally, there is the hotly debated issue of nutritional supplements for the mother. It has been widely held that the diet does not contain enough available iron to supply the needs of pregnancy and that therefore the pregnant woman will become iron deficient, with anaemia as the most obvious sign. That view was supported by changes in the blood, such as a falling haemoglobin concentration which suggested iron deficiency anaemia. We now know that a falling haemoglobin and all the other laboratory signs which ordinarily suggest deficiency are part of an elaborate readjustment of the body in pregnancy, and the evidence for iron deficiency is contentious. Even so, many will say, 'Why not take some iron anyway? It can't do any harm.' In fact, it can do harm and the sensible position taken now by many, perhaps most, obstetricians, is that the mother's blood should be examined from time to time in pregnancy and if she shows genuine signs of becoming anaemic then treatment is appropriate; blanket treatment of the whole pregnant population is not. The same can be said about folic acid, except that there is even less reason to expect healthy women in this country to be short of it.

What has been said here about nutritional supplements applies to a well-nourished European population. There are parts of the world where dietary deficiency of iron and folic acid is a serious public health problem and an extreme danger to the pregnant woman; there no one would disagree that it is wise to supplement all pregnant women. And there are groups in Britain where the same applies: for example, Asian women who customarily spend most of their time indoors with little exposure to sunlight, and women for whom calcium absorption may be impaired by an excess of cereals in the diet certainly benefit from regular supplementation of Vitamin D.

In conclusion, if you are healthy and well-nourished, relax and enjoy your pregnancy. Eat what you feel like, don't drink much alcohol (or smoke) and the baby who has millions of years of successful evolution behind him, will look after himself.

2
Miscarriage

Gordon H. Ramsden and
Peter M. Johnson

A pregnancy starts when a sperm fertilizes an egg; menstrual periods cease and the woman may notice both mental and physical changes. There is a sense of excitement, anticipation and that unique feeling of giving life to a being that is part of her, but yet an individual. Couples can expect and usually achieve a trouble-free pregnancy.

A miscarriage occurs when the pregnancy fails before the end of the twenty-seventh week. This may occur totally 'out-of-the-blue' or secondary to some specific reason. Emotional upheaval will often result: not only does the woman suffer from depression and grief, but often there are also feelings of disorientation, insecurity and guilt. She may start trying to reason with herself, blaming her career, age or lifestyle and is frequently unable to disclose or discuss her feelings. Her partner will also experience disappointment, and sometimes a feeling of uncertain failure, but these are often suppressed in the society of today as they may suggest weakness.

This chapter aims to explain some of the mystiques of miscarriage and assist the reader to formulate his or her own ideas.

Basic Physiology and Anatomy

The two fallopian tubes are attached to the uterus with the ovaries in close proximity (see Fig. 1). When an ovum is released, fertilization by sperm takes place as it enters the opening of the fallopian tube. Over the subsequent three to four days, the

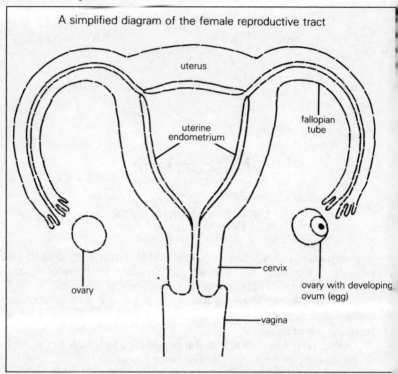

A simplified diagram of the female reproductive tract

uterus

uterine endometrium

fallopian tube

cervix

ovary

ovary with developing ovum (egg)

vagina

fertilized egg enlarges by multiplication of its cells and progresses down the tube to implant into the uterine endometrium, the lining of the womb. The developing embryo produces a hormone called human chorionic gonadotrophin (HCG) which stimulates the ovary to produce another hormone, progesterone, which stops the menstrual period. Once pregnancy has been established for about ten to twelve weeks, the production of progesterone by the ovary is thought to be less essential.

Incidence

Miscarriage is the commonest problem in pregnancy, occurring most often in the first twelve weeks. Indeed, it is likely that we all know of a friend or relative who has had one, two or more miscarriages. Miscarriages are known to occur in about one in six of established pregnancies. However, this may be an underestimate since recently more sensitive pregnancy testing, including blood tests as well as urine tests, suggest many pregnancies are lost around the implantation time (three to four days after fertilisation). In these cases, women may have a mistimed or heavier period, but could also notice nothing unusual from their normal menstrual cycle.

It is not commonly recognized that perhaps as many as one per cent of all couples suffer three or more consecutive miscarriages –a condition which obstetricians specifically refer to as 'recurrent miscarriage'. It is important, however, to stress that the vast majority of these women will be successful in achieving a normal full-term pregnancy.

Aetiology (Causes)

There are many possible causes of miscarriages and we will take each in turn.

Genetic
Each cell in the body of any individual has a 'control centre' called a nucleus. The information in any particular nucleus originates equally from both parents of that individual and is normally stored within the 46 chromosomes of the nucleus in subunits called genes. Before conception, however, the sperm and the egg each contain only 23 chromosomes; after conception, the combined 46 chromosomes form a 'new' nucleus which then controls cell growth and division, i.e. the entire development of the fetus (see Fig. 2).

The processes of sperm and egg production, and their fertilization, are delicate and may occasionally be disrupted. At fertilization, two sperm may enter the egg, giving rise instead to a total of 69 chromosomes. Cell multiplication in both the abnormal and normal conceptus can also result in chromosomes being lost or broken. Occasionally, there may be an extra chromosome present, making a total of 47, the commonest such condition being Down's Syndrome (Mongolism). The majority of these pregnancies will eventually present as a miscarriage, hence representing Nature's way of protecting against having an abnormally developed child. Some reports suggest that such chromosomal aberrations may be the underlying reason for up to fifty to sixty per cent of miscarriages occurring in the first twelve weeks of pregnancy. For most women, this is not a repeatedly inherited problem causing their miscarriage and hence they can look forward to a perfectly normal subsequent pregnancy. A small number of these women who suffer repeated miscarriages

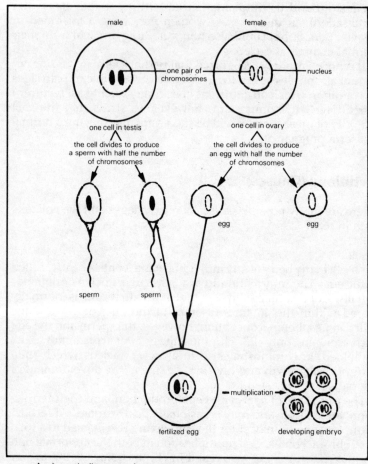

A schematic diagram to demonstrate normal egg and sperm production with subsequent fertilization. For simplification only one pair of chromosomes is demonstrated instead of the usual 23 pairs.

(about three per cent) have a slight abnormality of either their own or their partner's chromosomes, and it is possible to check for this by means of blood tests. An abnormality of one chromosome is not necessarily reflected in physical appearance, but may mean that the sperm or eggs do not contain the necessary full complement of genetic information for successful reproduction. The advice of a genetic counsellor can be sought in individual cases to explain the chances of a normal pregnancy.

Anatomic (physical)
During early development of the female fetus, the uterus is formed from the fusion of two separate tubes, and abnormal fusion can result in structural abnormalities ranging from a heart-shaped uterus to a double uterus. These different abnormalities would go undetected but may contribute in later life to either early or late miscarriages when pregnant. However, the clear association of an abnormally shaped uterus with persistent miscarriage is an unusual event. This may be suspected on vaginal examination, but needs to be confirmed by injecting dye through the cervix and performing an X-ray to demonstrate the shape of the uterine cavity. Other abnormalities may include fibroids and adhesions within the uterine cavity. Management of these problems may need surgery, and it would be necessary for the woman to discuss fully the implications with her obstetrician.

Cervical incompetence is a weakness of the neck of the womb, giving rise to either miscarriage after the first few months of pregnancy or to premature labour. Many obstetricians believe that this may be prevented by applying a stitch (cervical suture) to keep the cervix closed during pregnancy.

Hormonal
Of the many hormones characteristically produced in early pregnancy, the principal ones are human chorionic gonadotrophin (HCG) and progesterone. Research has suggested that some pregnancies fail because the progesterone level drops in early pregnancy. As progesterone production by the ovary is controlled by HCG, it would seem logical to give women either progesterone or HCG injections. Although many studies have been performed, results on the success of these injections vary considerably. This may be explained by the uncertainty as to whether it is the fall in progesterone which leads directly to the miscarriage or whether the miscarriage itself gives rise to the falling progesterone.

Occasionally, the mother's thyroid gland can be either under or over active and this can give rise to repeated miscarriages. This is easily checked by means of a blood test and may necessitate treatment.

Infections
Even the common cold has been blamed for sporadic miscarriages and, in individual cases, it is certainly difficult to prove or disprove. Rubella (German measles) is known to cause not only fetal abnormalities but also miscarriages. These risks have

been substantially reduced with the introduction of rubella vaccination. Certain other viral infections, such as genital herpes, may
give rise to miscarriages during the initial infection but uncertainty prevails over the effects of recurring infections. The
AIDS virus itself does not cause miscarriage, other than those
associated with general maternal illness.

Other infections, some of which are 'low-grade' in the mother,
have been cited as causing miscarriages. These include toxoplasmosis and mycoplasma, and can be detected by either blood
tests or cervical swabs. Treatment may be necessary in women
who have more than one miscarriage.

Medical
Diabetes, heart, lung and kidney disease, or a condition called
systemic lupus erythematosus (SLE), may either cause or otherwise be associated with miscarriages. Each individual woman has
to be fully assessed before a direct cause and effect can be
established. In most cases, the better control of the medical
condition is likely to increase the chance of success in pregnancy.

Immunological
Most people are aware of the immune system as providing
defence to infection, but it is also important in the context of
transplantation. Pregnancy involves a foreign tissue graft in the
uterus which, paradoxically, is not normally rejected by the
mother's immune system. Very recent studies have indicated
that, in occasional women, the immune system may not adapt as
normal to accepting the implanting embryo – the subsequent
'transplantation rejection' would be manifest as a miscarriage.
Although still in its infancy of research, there is much current
interest in this area, particularly for women suffering unexplained recurrent miscarriages. Several centres are in the
process of evaluating an immunization treatment and it is still too
early to give a precise idea of the strength of benefit or risk to this
approach. As with other causes of miscarriage, it is important
that specialist investigation is sought – perhaps more so in this
case since the relevant investigations to determine any immunological background presently remain somewhat uncertain. See
the following chapter for more information.

Other causes

Following any miscarriage, there is a natural tendency for a woman to try and establish a cause or reason. Those frequently blamed may include exercise, work, stress, long car journeys, moving house, sexual intercourse etc. None have necessarily been proven to give rise to miscarriages. In particular, sexual intercourse is not a cause of miscarriages although many women, understandably, may find this difficult to comprehend. However, anything in excess, namely exercise, stress and direct trauma to the stomach, may increase the risk of miscarriage.

Importantly, it is necessary to maintain a healthy diet, reduce or stop smoking and drinking, and have a moderate amount of exercise. If the woman feels well and the doctor is happy with her progress, there is no reason why she should not continue her normal daily activities including housework and career commitments. Should a woman have had problems with recurrent miscarriages then, on an empirical basis, rest either at home or hospital may be advised. A decision on the possible benefit is usually determined by discussion with the obstetrician and also consideration of domestic circumstances, e.g. young children at home. Chemotherapy (drugs) and radiotherapy (X-rays) may occasionally cause miscarriages, as well as fetal abnormalities, and women should ask about the risks to a pregnancy before accepting any investigations or drug treatment.

Signs and Symptoms of a Miscarriage

Miscarriage is the failure of a pregnancy before the end of the twenty-seventh week. There is a tendency for the medical profession to use the term spontaneous abortion rather than miscarriage, but this must not be confused with elective or therapeutic abortions.

A miscarriage is usually preceded by absent periods and the woman may have already noticed symptoms associated with pregnancy, such as nausea, vomiting, swelling, breast tenderness and tingling. With the onset of a miscarriage, there can be varying degrees of blood loss ranging from a small brownish discharge through to the passage of large clots. This loss may be accompanied by pain of increasing severity due to irritation of the uterus. Eventually, the woman may proceed into labour and the uterus succeed in expelling the conceptus. Approximately fifty per cent of pregnancies with some bleeding in the first twelve weeks will settle spontaneously and proceed normally to term. It is important to appreciate that such bleeding is usually from the edge of the developing placenta and is maternal in origin. Thus, a woman can be reassured that if the pregnancy continues and the bleeding settles, it is very unlikely that there will be any fetal damage in development. Occasionally, a miscarriage is detected on a routine ultrasound scan, showing either an empty gestational sac or blighted ovum or a non-viable pregnancy or missed abortion. The doctor would usually suggest a dilatation and curettage (D & C) which involves a short general anaesthetic and the tissue is gently removed from the uterus. This procedure does not jeopardize the woman's future fertility.

What should a woman do if she suspects she is having a Miscarriage?

Faced with a possible loss of one's baby, panic is a very natural reaction in any woman. Although obviously difficult, it is imperative for her to stay as calm as possible and consult a doctor at the earliest opportunity. Her doctor may recommend admission to hospital; this is principally for observation and, if necessary, pain relief. Hospital admission also gives more opportunity to discuss the situation with nursing and medical staff and, maybe also, with other women. She should not be alarmed if the doctor wishes to perform a vaginal examination; this will NOT damage the fetus or induce a miscarriage. The examination will enable the doctor to assess the age of the pregnancy, check that the pregnancy is not within a fallopian tube, and establish whether the neck of the womb is open or closed. If it is open and associated with heavy bleeding or the passage of products of conception, the doctor may again advise a D & C to remove any remaining tissue or clots. Should it be closed and bleeding slight, then an ultrasound scan is usually performed to establish the viability of the pregnancy. If the bleeding settles and the pregnancy continues, it is advisable to rest at home for a further week or two before gradually returning to normal activities.

What to do following a Miscarriage

Most women face two particular challenges after a miscarriage; firstly, coping with that period of time immediately after the miscarriage and, secondly, preparing both mentally and physically for any subsequent planned pregnancies (increased concern over which will be a natural response).

It is normal for a miscarriage to be followed by a period of reflection, sometimes together with a strong urge to get away for a short period from one's normal environment. Women's feelings can vary considerably and be influenced by the initial reaction to the pregnancy: thus, they may range from feelings of grief to almost euphoria. It is normal for a woman or a couple to try and rationalize the situation by establishing a cause for the miscarriage and blaming coincidental everyday events, of which few are proven to cause miscarriages. However, we would be wrong to be totally dismissive.

A priority is for the woman to feel able to express her feelings and ideas, and not to be frightened to seek reassurance and advice from family, friends and professionals. All too frequently, a sense of guilt is mixed with that of failure and this is further compounded by the expectations of modern society.

There are many established causes for miscarriages, as already indicated, and most occur as unfortunate isolated events which may be impossible to predict or prevent even with the advances in medical technology. Following miscarriages, the underlying cause may never become apparent and it is understandable that many women find this situation difficult to accept. The risk of a second consecutive miscarriage may be of the order of one in four, but the chance of a third pregnancy being successful after two consecutive miscarriages is still around seventy per cent. We realise that quoting such figures does not help the individual woman, but it is relevant to realize that miscarriages do not necessarily jeopardize future pregnancies. Indeed, we would emphasize that the vast majority of women who have suffered one, or even two miscarriages, are able to proceed subsequently to successful normal pregnancy.

There is, however, a very small minority of women who suffer more than three miscarriages. This may lead to feelings of despair and amplified emotional effects. Some couples may, where possible, elect for adoption although many couples will wish to understand the reasons for their repeated miscarriages. In this group of couples, more intensive investigations and counselling will be required. Our understanding of the various causes and treatments in recurrent miscarriages is steadily progressing, so that the chances of a subsequent successful pregnancy still remain good even with this unfortunate obstetric background.

There is a good argument for women to consult their doctor prior to starting or enlarging their family. This enables them to discuss their anxieties related to their general health or previous obstetrical experiences. The doctor may also take the opportunity to ask a few questions and perform a general examination which could involve some simple investigations or tests. Drug treatment may need to be altered and advice about health and diet is always available. This pre-pregnancy counselling is important and strongly advised in women with an established medical condition.

It is not possible here to address all questions, and the general practitioner is a useful source of further information. There is also an increasing number of hospital clinics dealing solely with the management of miscarriage patients. Nationally, there are several miscarriage support groups and further information can be obtained from the Miscarriage Association, 18 Stoneybrook Close, West Bretton, Wakefield, West Yorkshire WF4 4TP, Tel: 092-485-515.

3
Recurrent Miscarriage

J. F. Mowbray

The woman who suffers a single miscarriage goes through a very difficult time, and, in general, is told that it is just bad luck, and that there is nothing wrong, and that she should try again. This is an appropriate response for a first miscarriage but is very upsetting to the woman who suffers a second or third. She is sure that she has a problem, but gets the same bland reassurance that she obtained on the first occasion. What is her problem, how should it be identified and how does she get the appropriate treatment?

How Common is the Problem?

A recent study of healthy English women who were confirmed at five weeks as pregnant has shown that six in one hundred lose that pregnancy. The chance is the same whether this is their first pregnancy, or when they have had one or more live children born previously.

The chance of the next pregnancy also resulting in miscarriage is not significantly greater than the first, that is to say she still has a ninety to ninety-five per cent chance of success. When she has lost two pregnancies by miscarriage the chance of a third failing is somewhat higher, but she still will have a chance of success of more than seventy-five per cent. Three miscarriages do, however, distinguish the woman who has been very unlucky to have more than one miscarriage from the group of women with a real problem of recurrent miscarriage.

It is for the above reason that we only investigate, and treat where necessary, those women who have had three or more miscarriages. Those with only one or two do not usually need any special treatment, although they do need support and reassurance before and during their next pregnancy. The women who have recurrently miscarried represent only about one in four hundred women having children. They do need special investigation and treatment, as, after three miscarriages, their chance of a further miscarriage is high.

Causes of Repeated Miscarriage

Of the fifteen hundred or so couples with recurrent miscarriages that we have investigated and treated, there are a few causes which are common, and most of the couples' problems are due to a single cause. It is obviously of great importance to know that cause because it is unlikely that the couple will otherwise get the appropriate treatment for a successful pregnancy. It is necessary, therefore, that the couple are investigated carefully, and tests carried out to find what is the problem. Unfortunately in this area, it is very difficult to do tests that say 'This is the problem' Most of the tests that we carry out say instead 'this is normal, it is not the cause of the miscarriages'. One should then see that the process is really that of shutting doors to remove possible causes until one hopefully finds only a single door open. Then, and only then, is the couple likely to get appropriate treatment. Because, until the last few years, it has not been possible to make the appropriate tests, the general management has been to support the pregnancy with hormones and encouragement, without a clear idea of what was needed, and without a high degree of success. What then are the causes of recurrent miscarriage, and how can they be best managed?

When I first became involved in the immunological aspects of recurrent abortion, I thought that this cause would be a small part of the total. In the intervening ten years it has become clear that it is in fact the commonest cause, but other causes, particularly some inherited problems, also occur. Many of the abnormalities which were, and unfortunately sometimes still are, quoted as causes of repeated miscarriage are excuses, not real causes. The woman is investigated, and an 'abnormality' found which is blamed as the cause. It is my firm belief that there are only a very small number of common causes of the condition, and these can now largely be identified and treated appropriately. Below I have listed them, with a note about their identification and management. After this section we will consider some of the treatment which may be necessary in more detail.

Genetic Causes

As discussed in the previous chapter, single miscarriages quite frequently occur because of faults in the way that the egg and sperm fuse to produce the fertilized egg, and these faulty eggs may only be able to develop for a while, and then the embryos cannot develop further and a miscarriage occurs. This problem is one of single miscarriages, and would not occur three or more times in more than about one in eight thousand women. It is thus a very uncommon cause of recurrent miscarriage, but it does happen in a few older women. We have seen about ten examples in fifteen hundred couples with recurrent miscarriages. The risk of a single miscarriage from this genetic cause rises from about five per cent in the twenties to about ten to fifteen per cent by the fortieth year, and perhaps twenty-five per cent by age forty-five, although we have too few examples at that age to be very accurate.

The common genetic cause of repeated miscarriage is due to the baby's inheritance of faulty genes from the parents. The simplest example of this is one where each parent has, for a particular gene, one good copy and one bad one. The good copy keeps the parents healthy, and prevented their own miscarriage. Both parents pass only one copy to the offspring. Thus sometimes either parent may pass on a good gene, and sometimes a bad one. It is only on the occasions when a bad gene comes from *both* parents that there is trouble which results in miscarriage. It is obvious that this will only happen about once in four pregnancies. Both this kind of inheritance and another similar one will then only result in miscarriage of a fraction of the pregnancies, from a quarter to about a half. Thus the pattern seen is that of a mixture of successful pregnancies and miscarriages randomly occurring. This kind of genetic cause can then be suspected in a woman who produces a mixture of miscarriages and successful births, but not the women who miscarry all their pregnancies. In these a genetic cause is very unlikely.

To be told that the cause of recurrent miscarriages is genetic is to fear that this is a terrible untreatable problem, but in fact this is not the case. Some of the pregnancies will fail, because the fetus is defective, but other ones will produce *normal* children. If a couple has a known genetic problem which would produce abnormal children, geneticists may test each pregnancy and, if it is abnormal, suggest that it be terminated, and that the couple try again for a normal pregnancy. The woman with genetic cause for her miscarriages is carrying out her own 'planned terminations'. This is obviously as unpleasant as any other kind of miscarriage, but the woman is helped by knowing that the abnormal ones are lost, and that the children who develop and are born are the normal ones. Thus with persistence a couple with this problem may produce a healthy family but with a rather lower success rate than average.

It should be noted that the miscarriage rate in couples of this kind is not more than fifty per cent, and the burden of repeated miscarriage in order to produce a normal family is not intolerable. Although there is some variation in the time in pregnancy at which these genetic faults cause miscarriage, fortunately it is usually in the first three months. This reduces the hardship compared with a situation in which a pregnancy has gone to about twenty weeks before planned termination after an amniocentesis at about eighteen weeks to study the normality or otherwise of the fetus.

You may be able to see from the above that the outlook for the couple with common inherited faults is not totally disastrous; that they can be identified on their pattern of mixed normal and miscarrying pregnancies, and that with persistence they can produce further normal children. In these respects they are quite different from the other causes discussed below.

Infectious Causes
There are some infections which can cause a miscarriage, and one of these occurs quite commonly in Europe. This condition, called brucellosis, causes abortion in cattle and is spread by unpasteurized milk and milk products. It is not common in women with recurrent miscarriage, and although a woman infected may possibly have a single miscarriage, the infection does not persist to affect further pregnancies. The condition is readily treatable with antibiotics, as is the other condition which is called toxoplasmosis. This is not common in Europe, but occurs particularly in the Eastern Mediterranean and West Africa. Again most women infected are likely only to lose one pregnancy, and having cured themselves of the infection are resistant to reinfection. There are a small number of women, however, who have kept the infection for several pregnancies and have repeatedly miscarried. Treatment of the infection will prevent further miscarriages.

Anatomical Causes

It is not surprising that gynaecologists would look for structural abnormalities of the womb as possible causes of repeated miscarriage. On occasion they have found abnormalities, in particular partial or a complete double uterus, the condition called bicornuate uterus. Unfortunately as the condition is really only looked for in women with miscarriage it is not easy to discover how many normal women have this abnormality without problems.

We can say that a considerable number of women whose repeated miscarriages have been due to immunological causes have had successful pregnancies afterwards despite having a bicornuate uterus. An occasional miscarriage may be caused if the embryo implants on a thin dividing wall between the two parts of the uterus, but it is not a real cause of recurrent miscarriage. It is possible to repair the uterus surgically if it is really thought to be a problem.

Immunological Causes

It is now clear that there are two kinds of immunological abnormality leading to recurrent miscarriage. The first is due to the development of antibodies against some fatty substances present on some cell surfaces called phospholipids. The other is the common condition caused by failure of production of antibodies to paternal antigens which is now treated by immunization with paternal cells. These two forms are quite separate, and treatment is quite different for each.

a) Antibodies to phospholipids

It is only in the last two or three years that this condition has been recognized: that these antibodies can cause obstruction to the arteries of the uterus in pregnancy. This causes a failure of nutrition of the fetus so that growth is impaired, and miscarriage *after twenty weeks* may occur repeatedly. This condition is different therefore from recurrent miscarriages which happen mostly in the first three months. In all the women we have seen, half the miscarriages have occurred by eight weeks from their last period. This condition, in which miscarriages happen much later, or where small babies may be born after premature labour, is quite a separate pattern.

It has been possible to detect the antiphospholipid antibodies in many women with this condition, but sometimes they may only be found during pregnancy. It may then be necessary to test a woman at the start of her next pregnancy and then begin treatment if the antibody is found. Treatment was at first tried with drugs that are powerful at suppressing immune responses, but carried some risk in their use. Most groups are now safely treating this condition with aspirin and agents which prevent the reaction of the blood platelets to the antibody. We have used a combination of two, aspirin and heparin, from about the twelfth to the thirty-second week without any problems arising for the mother. Several combinations of drugs have been used success-fully to prevent further miscarriage, and to allow the develop-ment of babies of normal growth. Even with treatment a few women go into labour a little early, but with treatment the survival of the babies is high.

b) Lack of Antipaternal Antibodies

This is the last condition that we will consider, and is the cause of about three-quarters of all repeated miscarriage. Normally women recognize that the baby's cells possess antigens which come from the father. Half of the baby's antigens are, of course, from the woman herself, and she does not recognize these as 'foreign'. Unless the woman is protected, the foreign antigens will cause her to reject the fetus and placenta as a foreign tissue, in the way that she would a kidney transplant from another individual. This does not usually happen because the woman also makes antibodies which protect her from recognizing the fetus as foreign and damaging it. In about one couple in five hundred the woman is not immunized by the husband's antigens on the baby's cells, and thus she 'rejects' the pregnancy. Both husband and wife are normal, it is just the particular choice of partners which is the problem. With another partner the woman would make the antibodies normally. At present it seems that some kind of sharing of antigens between husband and wife reduces the ability of paternal antigens on the baby's cells to immunize the woman. She only sees half of the husband's antigens in any one pregnancy, and that is too weak to produce antibodies. When she is immunized with the husband's cells, which contain all his antigens, antibodies are made and she is then protected.

There has been a large amount of work on the immune reaction of the mother to her offspring, and many specific and non-specific protective factors have been identified in experimental animals. Many of the antibodies are now demonstrable in women as well, and their appearance in a normal pregnancy can be studied. Women with the problem of recurrent miscarriage have not usually made these antibodies, and this appears to be the reason for their miscarriages. Those women who do make normal antibodies of several kinds are likely to have another cause for their miscarriages. The antibodies which are usually measured are not necessarily the ones which are actually protective, but are the ones most easily identified in the blood. The now quite large number of medical groups treating this condition through the world, mostly agree that treatment by immunization is an effective treatment for those without antibodies, but should not be used for women with normal immunity. It is important therefore to establish that the woman lacks at least some of the normal antibodies before subjecting her to immunization treatment.

Treatment is available at about thirty centres in the world, and five or six of these are in the UK. Our centre, which is the largest, has now treated about a thousand couples with this immuno-logical form of recurrent miscarriage. Initially there was a success rate of about eighty per cent but this has risen somewhat in the last three years due to an improvement in identifying which women to treat, and improvements in some details of the immunization itself. The same sort of success is obtained by most other centres through the world, and although the majority use similar techniques to ours, other methods are also used.

We immunize the woman with blood lymphocytes from the husband on one occasion, plus a later booster injection for women who need it. Other groups may routinely use more than one dose of husband's cells. A few groups use white cells from blood donors, and one uses cell membrane preparations from other women's placentas.

There is still some controversy about the rationale for particular forms of treatment, but the high overall success rate, with large numbers of normal babies born, and without any hazard to the women apparent, has meant that this technique has come to stay as the main treatment of recurrent miscarriage.

It should be noted that one of the centres has used intensive psychotherapy to treat recurrent miscarriage, and has therefore obviously treated many women with immunological problems. They also have a high success rate, for unproven reasons, but probably ones related to the growth of placentas faster than the woman's immunity attacks them. The importance of this is, in part, that all of us who have tried to help couples with recurrent miscarriage recognize the importance of 'tender loving care' or TLC in their management. Possibly because the woman has suffered repeated disappointments after the elation of becoming pregnant there is a strong tendency for the woman (and her husband) sometimes to almost accept that miscarriage is inevitable. We try to support them by getting them to look at one day of the pregnancy at a time, and, although worrying, which is natural, *not* to assume that failure is going to occur. Obviously with some women this may be very time consuming, but the successful outcome makes that effort very worthwhile. Immunization is a very powerful tool of treatment, but the women treated are not all able to accept that 'things are going to be different this time'. The first three months of pregnancy are inevitably a time of great anxiety and to be able to see that another day has gone by and the pregnancy is still there is a great comfort. Monitoring the level of HCG, a placental hormone, and a scan at eight or nine weeks to show a baby growing normally and with a beating heart are additional strong supports to the woman.

Help for a couple suffering from recurrent miscarriages is not then just 'high tech', but also demands an understanding of the woman as an individual with entirely comprehensible fears and emotions, and this understanding is essential to help her through the early months of the pregnancy.

4

Uncontrolled Division of Cells at Conception: Hydatidiform Mole and its Possible Consequences

Peter Howie

Hydatidiform mole is a condition which occurs in about one in two thousand women in Britain who become pregnant. To begin with, the women have every reason to suspect that they are expecting a baby. They will have missed a period and their pregnancy tests will have been strongly positive. They will have experienced many of the classic signs of pregnancy, perhaps feeling that they are bigger than they would expect for their dates and often having particularly bad morning sickness. Frequently however these women will experience bleeding in the early weeks of their pregnancy and think that they are having a miscarriage.

But when the woman is examined, no fetal heart is heard and no fetal parts can be detected with an ultrasound scan. On scan, all that can be seen is a number of white echoes in the uterus which gives a 'snowstorm' appearance. Testing of the mother's blood will reveal vastly elevated levels of the hormone classically used to diagnose pregnancy, human chorionic gonadotrophin (HCG).

On the basis of the scan and the hormone tests, the woman will be told that a hydatidiform mole has been diagnosed. 'Mole' in this context has nothing to do with a mole on the skin (or for that matter a garden mole) – it simply means 'a mass'. 'Hydatid' means a clear fluid-filled cyst – so, taken together, the term refers to a mass consisting of fluid-filled cysts. In fact, a mole that looks like a bunch of clear filled grapes. One reason why this condition is a cause for concern is that, in about six to ten per cent of cases, it may develop into a particular type of cancer called chorio-carcinoma. Thirty years ago, this cancer had a very poor prognosis but happily, research has transformed this situation. This disease called choriocarcinoma, which was once so devast-ating, is now nearly always amenable to complete cure in this country – but only because of diligent monitoring of all those women who have had a hydatidiform mole. It is usual to regard a mole as being a benign form of trophoblastic disease which, as a potentially malignant condition, may proceed to the frankly malignant (or cancerous) disorder of choriocarcinoma. But what is trophoblast or indeed trophoblastic disease? To understand this condition, it is necessary to know a little about the very early stages of pregnancy.

Soon after conception, rapid division of the fertilized egg takes place, so that very quickly a ball of cells is formed. The outer layer of these cells is called the trophoblast and is responsible for the early nutrition of the embryo but it rapidly develops, with other cells, into a sort of double envelope, the outer layer of which is called the chorion. The bits of the trophoblast/chorion sandwich are pushed out, forming little finger-like projections of cells called trophoblastic villi (from the Latin villus meaning finger). At this stage the early pregnancy looks a bit like a sputnik. Once in contact with the wall of the uterus, these little fingers of trophoblast can, by enzyme action, burrow into the cells of the uterus, thus gaining an anchorage point on the uterine wall. Only some of the projections on the 'sputnik', those which are in contact with the uterine wall, will develop into the placenta. All the others (those that point into the uterine cavity and which will not be used), will later waste away. Collection of these super-fluous trophoblastic villi, before they atrophy, is the basis of chorionic villus sampling (CVS) which is discussed in Chapter 5 by Dr Nicolaides.

Trophoblast is potentially very invasive stuff, and, from one point of view, this is good because it favours as large a development of placenta as possible. However, how does it know when to stop, and what happens if the trophoblast doesn't function properly? A mole is formed when part, or all of the trophoblast gets out of control and undergoes degenerative changes. No fetal development is possible so the conceptus remains as an undifferentiated ball of cells. Sometimes enough proper placental tissue persists to nourish an embryo through the early stages of development but usually the whole of the trophoblast is involved and the embryo is absorbed. Thus moles are diagnosed as being either complete or partial depending on whether the whole or only part of the trophoblast is involved.

Who Gets a Mole and Why?

Throughout the world, many studies have uncovered several striking features connected to the epidemiology of hydatidiform moles. Although moles occur in about one in two thousand pregnancies in Britain, in Asian countries such as Indonesia and the Philippines the incidence may rise to one in two hundred pregnancies. However immigrant Filipino women in America have a similar incidence to the rest of the American population leading to the conclusion that differences in its occurrence are geographical or environmental rather than racial. There is also a strong association of incidence with age – being increased in women under twenty years of age and rising very sharply after the age of forty and especially after the age of fifty. There seems to be no link between moles and either diet or social deprivation. If a woman has had one molar pregnancy she has a greater risk of a further mole than other women. However, the risk of a second mole is actually only very slightly increased, by less than two per cent in fact, so that most women are subsequently able to have a normal family.

Recently it has been discovered, from chromosome analysis of the cells making up the mole, that complete moles have no chromosome element from the mother at all. Normally of course, both mother and father provide equal quantities of genetic material. It seems that in a complete mole, a sperm in effect fertilizes an 'empty egg' – one that has no maternal chromosomes in it – so subsequent cell division just leads to duplication of the father's chromosomes. In a partial mole, two sperms fertilize an egg and join with the maternal chromosomes giving a double complement of paternal chromosomes and a single complement of maternal ones. The common factor in complete and partial moles seems to be a double complement of paternal chromosomes, with the complete mole also lacking any maternal chromosomes. This is clearly abnormal so it can be seen that this problem is one that literally arises at the moment of conception. Complete moles, that is those where no trace of fetal tissue can be found, have more potential to be malignant than partial moles so that follow up is particularly important after complete moles. However, although the distinction between partial and complete mole sounds distinct, in practice it is sometimes difficult for the pathologist to decide which type of mole it is. If there is any doubt, full follow up is arranged on the assumption that it may be a complete mole. If it is clear that a partial mole has been present only a shorter period of follow-up is necessary.

What happens once a Mole is Diagnosed?

Once a mole has been diagnosed, evacuation of the uterus is the first priority, the aim being to eliminate all abnormal tropho-blastic tissue from the maternal system. Even if a spontaneous abortion has already occurred, suction curettage is still necessary to make sure that the uterus is completely empty. Because trophoblast is so well supplied with blood vessels, haemorrhage is always a risk and access to appropriate transfusion services is essential at the time of operation. With specialist services, however, evacuating a mole is nearly always accomplished without difficulties.

One possible consequence of having a mole is that of tropho-blast tissue escaping elsewhere in the body via the mother's bloodstream and adhering to other organs such as the lungs. This sounds worse than it is and in fact, with appropriate drug treatment, the trophoblastic tissue can be dissolved away and the prognosis is good. The main consequence however is the development of choriocarcinoma and this occurs in about six to ten per cent of those with molar pregnancy.

It is obviously difficult to know whether all the trophoblast tissue has been removed at the time of the evacuation of the uterus. Thirty years ago, one just had to guess and hope. But this chapter started by saying that high levels, usually in excess of 100,000 international units, of the hormone associated with pregnancy, HCG, were diagnostic of molar pregnancy. After a mole has been evacuated, HCG levels usually fall to normal levels within a few weeks. If, however, all the trophoblast tissue has not been removed or if a small remaining piece later becomes active, the level of HCG secreted by the woman in her body fluids will fail to fall or will rise even further – thus providing an excellent diagnostic test. In order to prevent problems, the earliest possible diagnosis of choriocarcinoma is essential. This is why follow-up for two years is recommended to all women who develop a hydatidiform mole.

Follow Up

All women who have had a mole are registered through the Royal College of Obstetricians and Gynaecologists. Three centres in Britain, Charing Cross Hospital, the Jessop Hospital in Sheffield and Ninewells Hospital in Dundee offer a postal follow-up service whereby, at appropriate intervals, containers for urine are sent to the patient who returns a sample for analysis. The results are sent back to the patients' own consultants and general practitioners. The three units endeavour to ensure that no patient is lost to follow-up. If HCG levels rise during the period of surveillance, usually at monthly or two monthly intervals over two years, it could be because of a subsequent pregnancy so this possible cause is investigated by doing a scan. Patients are advised to avoid pregnancy until follow-up has been completed as this could cause confusion of results and the diagnosis of choriocarcinoma might be missed. Effective contraception is essential and the pill can be used. In the minority with evidence of persistent trophoblastic disease early diagnosis of chorio-carcinoma ensures a very good prognosis with complete cure in almost every case. The development of this effective system of follow-up has been largely responsible for the dramatic fall in the number of women dying of choriocarcinoma to practically zero.

Choriocarcinoma

In the great majority of cases (over ninety per cent), all tests for HCG during the two year follow-up are negative and, at the end of this time, the woman can be reassured that all is well and can be allowed to try for a further baby, if she so wishes. Happily choriocarcinoma is rare in this country (only one in four thousand pregnancies) but once again, it is much more common in Asia. The risk of choriocarcinoma is a thousand times greater after a molar pregnancy than after a normal one and much more likely to occur after a complete mole than a partial mole.

In choriocarcinoma, the cancerous trophoblast rapidly invades the lining of the womb and transfers itself to other sites such as the lung, brain and liver. Clinical features, besides the elevated levels of HCG, are varied but can include vaginal haemorrhage, abdominal swelling (from the increasing tumour mass) and no periods.

If diagnosis is made at an early stage, the prognosis is very favourable and a survival rate of at least ninety-seven per cent is expected when the interval between the antecedent pregnancy and the onset of chemotherapy is less than four months. Thirty years ago, the prognosis was appalling and the disease was almost invariably fatal. The mainstay is treatment with anti-cancer drugs, which dissolve away the malignant tissue. The normal drug is called methotrexate, which can be given in differing regimes with other drugs depending on whether the patient has been allocated to a low, medium or high risk category. The differing regimes are intended to overcome possible drug resistance. As with all anti-cancer drugs, some side effects can occur and these depend upon the drug regime which is used. Treatment is given in specialized centres and, before treatment, the doctor in charge will explain what effects may be expected and what can be done to overcome them. After treatment is over, the side effects will resolve and the woman can expect to return to full health. Before the introduction of chemotherapy, hysterect-omy was the only treatment but now the aim is not only to overcome the cancer completely but to allow women to have subsequent pregnancies should they wish. A remarkable turn around for a disease that was the cause of such dread for patients and obstetricians such a relatively short while ago – and surely one of the most compelling success stories of modern research in obstetrics.

5
Monitoring the Fetus in Pregnancy

Kypros H. Nicolaides and Robert J. Bradley

The aim of antenatal care is to supervise closely the course of pregnancy in order to achieve the satisfactory delivery of a healthy baby. The majority of complications that arise in pregnancy are difficult to predict, and it is usually impossible to identify at the first visit to the antenatal clinic, either by careful history taking or by physical examination, those pregnancies that will not take a normal course. Antenatal care, therefore, is designed to identify those pregnancies that are most likely to develop problems, and detect those problems sufficiently early on to allow appropriate intervention. A variety of methods are available to do this.

Is the Baby Normal?

Advances in technology during the last decade have resulted in the ability to detect many fetal abnormalities during pregnancy, and to offer parents the option of abortion, although it is now possible to correct some of these abnormalities either before or after birth. The abnormalities that may occur fall roughly into three groups.

Fetal malformations
These are structural abnormalities that arise during the development of the fetus. They cover a wide range of conditions, such as spina bifida (where the skin covering the nerves in the spine is not complete) and 'holes in the heart' (where the muscular walls separating the chambers of the heart fail to join properly). Although some conditions may be inherited, the majority of

malformations develop without anyone else in the family being affected.

Chromosomal abnormalities
These include a number of conditions, the best-known of which is Mongolism (Down's Syndrome), which is due to the presence of extra chromosomes in every cell of the affected individual's body. Normally each cell in the human body contains 46 chromosomes (present as 23 matching pairs), which are situated in the nucleus of each cell. These chromosomes are made up of thousands of genes, which are responsible, not only for the inheritance of characteristics such as eye colour, but also for the regulation of how each cell functions within the body. Mistakes may occur in the way the chromosomes are passed from the parents to the fetus at fertilization, in which case the baby may carry the wrong number of chomosomes, or it may inherit chromosomes that have become damaged.

The effect of chromosomal abnormalities varies tremendously depending on the nature of the defect. They may result in structural malformations, such as those mentioned already, and therefore would be detected by ultrasound ocanning. Unfortunately, however, most chromosomal abnormalities do not cause malformations so the majority are not usually diagnosed until birth, when babies are found to be mentally handicapped.

As with the fetal malformations, most chromosomal abnormalities occur without any previous history of the condition in the family. Methods are available to diagnose these abnormalities early in pregnancy, but because these tests carry a risk of causing a miscarriage, they are generally only offered to couples especially at risk of having an affected child. The risk increases with maternal age, and the most common abnormality, though by no means the only one, is Mongolism. The reason for this increasing incidence is that all the eggs in a woman's ovaries are formed when she herself is a fetus, so at the age of forty, for example, the egg released at ovulation is forty years old. Something about the age of the egg predisposes it to behave abnormally, thus increasing the chance of passing too few or too many chromosomes on to the fetus. In most centres prenatal testing of the baby's chromosomes is offered to any woman over the age of thirty-five years. Sperm, on the other hand, is constantly being formed throughout a man's life, so increasing paternal age carries no extra risk to the fetus.

Familial and metabolic disorders

These are a group of conditions where although the right number of chromosomes are present, some of the genes on those chromosomes are abnormal (resulting in, for example, sickle cell disease, thalassaemia, haemophilia, muscular dystrophy, cystic fibrosis). These are all inherited disorders, but frequently the parents may be unaware that they carry the abnormal gene. This is because chromosomes are present in pairs, and if the abnormal gene is on only one chromosome of the pair, the individual is not usually affected himself, but is merely a 'carrier'. If, on the other hand, the abnormal gene is on both chromosomes of a pair, then the individual will suffer the ill effects of the disease. Thus, if both mother and father are 'carriers' there is a chance that their child will inherit the abnormal gene from each parent, and will therefore suffer from the disease. Many such parents, unfortunately, are not diagnosed as carriers until they have had an affected child.

The carrier state in many of these conditions can be diagnosed, and if couples are known to be at risk (e.g. sickle cell disease amongst the black population), or one partner has a family history of an inherited disorder (e.g. haemophilia), they should be tested before starting a family. They should then be advised of the risks of having an affected child, and of the tests available to diagnose the condition antenatally.

Ultrasound

Modern ultrasound machines allow the prenatal detection of the majority of structural malformations. Because it is usually impossible, however, to identify couples who are likely to have a malformed child, every pregnant woman should be offered an ultrasound scan at an early enough stage for an abortion to be performed if necessary. We now do a scan routinely at approximately twenty weeks of pregnancy, as this is the earliest stage at which we can best diagnose both serious malformations and more subtle defects, such as hare-lip or mild dilatation of the kidneys. Although these are not serious in themselves, they may alert us to the possible presence of serious chromosomal defects, and we can then carry out further tests which may identify them before birth.

Tissue Sampling

In order to diagnose non-structural abnormalities in the fetus, it is necessary to take a sample of tissue for analysis, a biopsy. This can be done in three ways.

Amniocentesis

Once the fetus forms within the uterus, it is contained in a bag or sac of amniotic fluid, rather like a fairground goldfish. This fluid is formed from the baby's urine and is constantly being swallowed and replaced by the fetus throughout pregnancy. Amniotic fluid also contains living cells shed from the baby's skin, as well as various chemicals produced by the baby, so that if analysed it gives valuable information about the fetus.

Amniocentesis is the technique by which samples of amniotic fluid are taken, and can be used at any stage of pregnancy from approximately sixteen weeks. An ultrasound scan is used to identify a pool of fluid, clear of the placenta, then a needle is passed through the mother's abdomen into the amniotic sac to take the sample. The skin where the needle goes in is rubbed with an antiseptic solution, but she is not given a local anaesthetic for this procedure, since most women find that injection more uncomfortable than the amniocentesis itself. The operator holds the scan probe in one hand and guides the needle with his or her other hand, so it is monitored throughout by the scan, to avoid it injuring either the placenta or the baby (see illustration in chapter 6) in the process. Nevertheless, there is a slight risk of miscarriage with amniocentesis: it happens in about one per cent of cases.

Chromosome analysis is the most common reason for performing this test, although a wide range of disorders can also be diagnosed. It is offered to couples who have chromosomal defects themselves, a family history of a chromosomal abnormality that may recur, or on the grounds of maternal age.

The test itself is quick, but the results take from between four to five weeks. This is because there are relatively few living cells in the amniotic fluid so they have to be grown, or multiplied, in a laboratory to get enough cells to give a reliable result, and this is what takes time. Problems may arise during this process, either because the cells fail to grow in culture, or because the analysis may identify different groups of cells, each with a different chromosome content. This last finding is particularly difficult to interpret, because it may have arisen in two ways. It could indicate a fetal condition known as mosaicism, where the fetus is literally a mosaic of cells containing different numbers of chromosomes, and which is associated with varying degrees of mental and physical handicap. Alternatively, it may have arisen spontaneously amongst otherwise normal cells during the laboratory culture. The only way to know is to take another sample of amniotic fluid or fetal blood and start again.

In Britain maternal blood is tested in the first half of pregnancy for a chemical known as alphafetoprotein. Although this chemical is present in the blood of all pregnant women, high levels may be associated with a variety of fetal malformations including spina bifida. However, only one in every fifteen women with a raised level of alphafetoprotein will have an abnormal baby, and therefore further investigations are necessary before it can be confirmed. Hospitals with good ultrasound facilities will use scanning to look for further abnormalities, but centres without the necessary expertise and equipment will analyse the amniotic fluid with an amniocentesis.

Placental Biopsy (chorionic villus biopsy)
The placenta starts to form as soon as the early fetus attaches itself to the wall of the uterus. Its main functions are to receive food and oxygen from the mother, and to excrete waste products from the fetus. Because the placenta develops from the same egg and sperm as the fetus, analysis of cells from the placenta provides the same information as analysis of cells from the fetus itself. Samples may be taken from the placenta from as early as eight weeks, and because there are many more actively growing cells than in a sample of amniotic fluid, the results should be back within two to three weeks.

Initially we obtained these samples through the cervix (neck of the womb), but because of the difficulty in sterilizing the vagina and the indignity experienced by the mother placing her legs in stirrups for the procedure, we now biopsy the placenta transabdominally using a similar technique to that for amniocentesis. The operator holds the scanner in one hand and guides a needle with the other hand through the mother's skin into the uterus and, without puncturing the bag of amniotic fluid, draws off a few fragments of placental tissue with a syringe. This procedure takes a little longer than an amniocentesis, so local anaesthetic is usually used to numb the skin beforehand. Although the miscarriage rate after placental biopsy is often quoted as three to four per cent, the risk of the test itself causing a miscarriage is actually 0.5 to one per cent, which is comparable with amniocentesis. The risk of any pregnant woman miscarrying between eight and twelve weeks of pregnancy is roughly two to three per cent, and this figure is often mistakenly added to the real risk factor of 0.5 to one per cent due to the placental biopsy itself.

In order to diagnose some inherited conditions from placental tissue samples, it is necessary first to analyse blood samples from the parents and any affected members of the family. This may take some weeks and should be performed before conception for couples at risk of inherited disorders such as thalassaemia, cystic fibrosis and Duchenne muscular dystrophy. Any couple with a family history of such conditions should contact their doctor for advice before starting a family.

Fetal blood sampling
Most inherited disorders can be diagnosed by the analysis of pure fetal blood. Indeed, some disorders may only be confidently diagnosed on these samples, such as mosaicism and fragile-X syndrome, a condition resulting in mental retardation in male babies. The first method used to take fetal blood was fetoscopy. This involved inserting a fine telescope into the uterus and, under direct vision, puncturing one of the blood vessels in the umbilical cord, and withdrawing a small sample of the baby's blood. However, this means heavy sedation, a couple of days' stay in hospital and carries a relatively high risk of causing a leak of amniotic fluid. It therefore has been largely replaced by another technique, namely cordocentesis. This involves the puncture of the umbilical cord where it attaches to the placenta. It is essentially the same technique as for amniocentesis and placental biopsy; the needle is guided by ultrasound, it takes only a few minutes, and the mother can return home immediately afterwards. The risk of miscarriage is also approximately one per cent.

Cordocentesis may be used to obtain fetal blood from eighteen weeks onwards. The major advantage of the technique is that because analysis of blood samples is so rapid, most conditions can be diagnosed within one week. This means that not only is parental anxiety minimized by a shorter wait for results, but also that the procedure may be used at later stages in pregnancy while abortion is still available as an option. This could be useful if the mother has booked into the antenatal clinic late, or if an amniocentesis culture fails. Also, the access that cordocentesis provides into the circulation of the fetus means that not only can blood be taken from the baby, it can also, in the case of rhesus disease, be given by transfusion during pregnancy. The survival rate for these babies thus becomes greater than ninety per cent.

Is the Baby Growing?

One of the main aims of antenatal care is to assess the growth of the fetus. If a small baby is found, it may be attributed to a number of causes, and further investigation is necessary. The baby may be small simply because the parents are small or are of a racial group, such as Asian, which tends to have relatively small babies, in which case there is no cause for concern. Alternatively, it may be small because it is not receiving all the nutrition it should from the placenta, which is called uteroplacental insufficiency, and which could result in fetal distress or even stillbirth. Occasionally the baby may be small because it is abnormal, and in certain cases the tissue sampling methods described earlier may be used for fetal chromosomal analysis. Obviously these three groups carry very different implications for the baby and its parents.

If the doctor suspects that the baby is small from measuring the height of the uterus while examining the mother's abdomen, then an ultrasound scan should be performed to confirm the suspicion, as the examination in the clinic is not a very accurate way of assessing fetal growth. By taking a variety of measurements with the scanner, it may be possible to identify whether or not the baby is suffering from growth retardation due to uteroplacental insufficiency. With the use of a special kind of ultrasound, Doppler (see p. 39), the blood supply to the placenta and to the fetus can also be measured. This may help make the identification and monitoring of these cases more accurate. It may also indicate the level of oxygen in the baby's blood.

Is the Baby Well?

Most complications of pregnancy that may compromise fetal well-being cannot be anticipated, either from the mother's history or by examination in early pregnancy. However, some pre-existing disorders are known to have potentially adverse effects on the fetus, e.g. heart disease, hypertension (high blood pressure), kidney disease and diabetes. In these conditions, or when complications arise for the first time in pregnancy, the assessment of fetal well-being is an important part of antenatal monitoring.

Fetal Growth

In general a baby that is growing well is well. However, as discussed above, the discovery of a small baby in pregnancy does not necessarily indicate a baby at risk from uteroplacental insufficiency. Mothers with babies that are growth retarded due to uteroplacental insufficiency are usually admitted to hospital for close monitoring, and serial ultrasound measurements, performed every two weeks, may be used to assess whether growth is continuing. Daily fetal heart rate tracing is carried out to assess the baby's well-being, and if Doppler ultrasound is available, it may also be used to assess its condition. A decrease or cessation in fetal growth, or a worsening in the Doppler measurements will usually prompt delivery of the baby. These methods are discussed in the sections following.

Fetal Movements

Fetal activity has long been used as a marker of fetal well-being, but may be unreliable. Towards the end of pregnancy it is usual for mothers to report a decrease in their baby's movements, presumably due to a lack of free space within the uterus. This decline is usually gradual and does not indicate any problem with the baby. In addition, the appreciation of fetal movements differs greatly between different mothers and different pregnancies. It is therefore unhelpful for one woman to compare her baby's movements with other mothers, or with her own previous experience. What is more helpful is the trend of movements in the present pregnancy, and 'kick charts' may be kept by the mother to detect any significant decline in activity. In some hospitals these charts are issued to every woman in late pregnancy, while in others only to those with complications. An abrupt decline or cessation in fetal movements should immediately be brought to the attention of the midwife or doctor for further assessment.

Fetal Heart Monitoring

The introduction of electronic fetal heart monitors, or cardiotocography, has enabled a much more sensitive assessment of fetal well-being than could be achieved by listening alone. Inspection of the print-out (CTG) from the machine, both before and during labour, is a fairly accurate method of monitoring the baby's condition. The heart trace is assessed by its rate in beats per minute, the presence or absence of accelerations or decelerations (where the rate respectively increases or decreases for a brief period) and the variation in the heart rate from beat to beat (the heart beat is usually irregular).

Electronic monitors should be used as part of the assessment of any pregnancy in which complications arise, but their routine use in every labour has been decried in certain quarters and may well be unnecessary. However, it is not possible to predict which apparently normal labours will develop problems, and for this reason some practitioners advocate their use universally.

While a 'good trace', with a normal rate (accelerations and no decelerations), is very reassuring that all is well, an 'abnormal trace' does not necessarily represent fetal difficulties. If it is severely abnormal, however, it does mean the baby should be delivered by the fastest method available. If the trace is only mildly abnormal, the baby's condition should be more closely assessed first. This is done by taking a fetal blood sample by pricking the baby's scalp, which may easily be seen through the open cervix during labour. Immediate analysis of this sample will tell if the trace truly represents any fetal distress and whether the baby should be delivered.

Biochemical Assessment

The original method of assessing fetal well-being was to measure the mother's urine or blood levels for various chemicals produced by the placenta, such as oestriol or human placental lactogen (HPL). While these methods may be useful, they have been generally replaced by the use of ultrasound scanning in centres where the necessary expertise is available.

Doppler Ultrasound

If sound is directed from an observer at an object, the sound will bounce off that object back to the observer, like an echo. If the object is moving, either towards or away from the observer, then the sound returning to the observer will be either higher or lower pitched than the sound that was directed at the object. For example, if a police car is driving towards you with the siren on, the sound becomes higher pitched until it reaches you and then becomes lower pitched as it drives away. This change in the pitch of the sound is called the 'Doppler effect'. The principle of Doppler has been put to many uses, the most familiar of which is in motoring 'speed traps', where a beam of sound, too high to be heard, is directed at a moving car. The sound that bounces off the car is received by the machine, which measures the pitch change, and from that change can calculate the speed of the car.

Recently, Doppler ultrasound has been employed to monitor fetal well-being. As described earlier, the fetus receives nutrition and oxygen from the mother across the placenta. Blood from the mother flows into the part of the uterus to which the placenta is attached. As it flows past the placenta, oxygen and nutrients cross the thin membrane that separates the mother's blood from the baby's. Obviously, if the mother's blood is flowing past the placenta in a fast, continuous stream it will deliver more oxygen to the baby than if the flow is sluggish. With the use of Doppler it is possible to measure this flow, and in cases of fetal growth retardation due to uteroplacental insufficiency these flows are often decreased. The blood flow within the baby itself may also be measured, and we have found that the speed of the blood flowing in the large blood vessels is a useful measure of the oxygen levels in the baby. Therefore, in cases of uteroplacental insufficiency, Doppler may be used to detect any deterioration in the oxygen supply to the baby, and allow delivery before the heart trace becomes severely abnormal. The routine use of Doppler may also allow us to predict those babies that will not grow normally in later pregnancy, as in some cases it appears that the flows may be abnormal even before the baby's growth slows down. This application may be especially useful in those cases where there has been a previous stillbirth due to uteroplacental insufficiency, as it may detect signs of the same problem recurring before the growth of the fetus is affected.

Fetal Blood Sampling

The method of obtaining fetal blood during pregnancy has enabled the more direct study of fetuses in high-risk pregnancy. For example, analysis of samples from babies that are growth retarded as a result of uteroplacental insufficiency has shown that some are short of oxygen, and these findings may alter the management of these cases. These techniques are also being employed to study the behaviour of babies in pregnancies complicated by maternal diabetes.

Conclusion

The use of all these techniques for monitoring the fetus in pregnancy means that we are now able to recognize the majority of fetal abnormalities at an early stage. Their application in later pregnancy allows closer assessment of the baby's well-being than ever before, and greatly assists in the successful delivery of a healthy baby.

6

Ultrasound in Pregnancy

J. M. Pearce

Ultrasound examinations have been used for the past twenty-five years in the management of pregnancy. In the past ten years, however, the equipment has become more advanced and cheaper so that most hospitals now offer one or more often two ultrasound examinations during the course of a woman's pregnancy. The first examination is designed to determine if the baby is the correct size for its age; to see if it is normal; and to diagnose twins. A second scan may be offered later in pregnancy to determine the size of the baby. If you have a complication in pregnancy your obstetricians may order serial ultrasound scans to look in detail at your baby's growth. Up to now ultrasound examinations have not been shown to harm mother or baby and they will provide many otherwise unobtainable benefits. Ultrasound examinations are often known as scans, ultrasounds or ultrascan. For the rest of this chapter they will be referred to as scans.

What is Ultrasound?

Ultrasound is sound of a higher pitch than can be heard by the human ear. When ultrasound is directed into the human body it produces echoes from interfaces between differing tissues. These echoes are returned to a computer which constructs a picture on a television screen. This is rather like a submarine using sonar to determine the depth and the shape of the bottom of the ocean.

The older ultrasound machines were large and involved a crane-like structure. They required a great deal of skill to operate and only produced a static picture; this meant that the operator

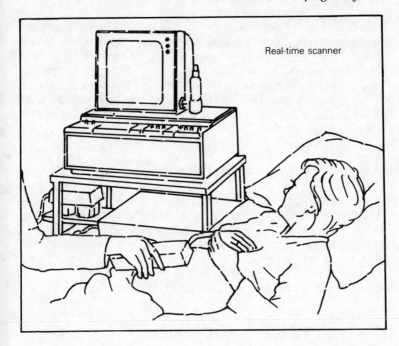

Real-time scanner

and the mother could not see the baby moving on the screen. The newer machines are called realtime ultrasound. Essentially these still produce static pictures but the picture is changed so rapidly that movements of the baby and of the baby's heart may be observed.

More recently Doppler ultrasound has been used to study pregnancy. In this situation ultrasound is used to detect moving structures. Ultrasound is directed towards the moving structure and the returning echo undergoes a shift in tone. This is called the Doppler effect (see page 39) and by using it, ultrasound blood flow to the afterbirth and within the baby may be studied.

What will my visit to the Scan Department involve?

In early pregnancy you will be asked to attend the scan department with a full bladder. This involves drinking a pint of water approximately one hour before you arrive. This is necessary because the womb normally lies behind the bones of the pelvis and a full bladder will push the womb out of the pelvis.

Once inside the department you will be asked to lay down on a trolley and lower your skirt and underclothes. In some departments you may be given the opportunity of changing into a hospital type of gown. As ultrasound will not travel through air it is necessary to cover your skin with a gel. The moveable part of the scan will be placed on your skin and you will see a picture on the television screen. The scan is painless and aside from the wet, sticky nature of the gel and the slight pressure of the scan head it is not uncomfortable.

When will I have my first Scan?

Most hospitals now offer the first scan sixteen to eighteen weeks after the first day of your last period. Although this often means an additional visit to hospital the baby will now be fully formed and measurements and examination of the baby are most accurate at this stage. Some hospitals still offer an ultrasound examination at the time of antenatal booking. If this is so, it is usually carried out for the convenience of the patient.

What will my first Scan tell me?

The age of your baby
The person performing the scan will measure your baby and will compare the measurements with the age of your baby as worked out by you, your obstetrician or your GP from the first day of your last period. If you are unsure about the first day of your last period, or if it is considered to be unreliable because your periods are irregular, or you have been recently taking the oral contraceptive pill or you have had bleeding in early pregnancy then the scan is the only accurate way of determining the age of the baby.

Even if you are sure about the first day of your last menstrual period a scan will more accurately predict the date at which you should deliver. This is extremely important as most obstetricians still prefer to induce labour in women whose pregnancy has exceeded the expected date of delivery by two weeks or more. The scan determines the age of the baby by size, which is more precisely related to the actual date of conception. Inaccuracies occur in working out the age of the baby and, therefore, the expected date of delivery, by using the first day of your last menstrual period since this method assumes that conception occurs two weeks after that period. This is not always the case and many women conceive a little later (or earlier) in the cycle.

Performing routine scans in early pregnancy will therefore produce more accurate expected dates of delivery and reduce by approximately a half the number of women whose pregnancies exceed their estimated date of delivery by two weeks or more. This means that if you have your pregnancy dated correctly by scan you are less likely to be advised that labour needs to be induced.

If at the time of your scan the person performing the examination tells you that your dates are wrong do not get upset. All this means is that you probably conceived your baby a little earlier or later than would be suggested by using the date of your last menstrual period as a method of predicting your baby's size or the estimated date of delivery. Very occasionally the size of the baby may disagree with that predicted from the first day of your last menstrual period by as much as a month or more. In these cases it is usually because there has been some bleeding in early pregnancy which you have assumed was a period. The baby is very rarely small for its dates at this stage and therefore it is safe to alter your expected date of delivery to that predicted by the scanned size of the baby.

Will my first Scan tell me that my Baby is Normal?

If you have had an abnormal baby before or have a history of abnormal babies in your family you will probably be sent to an expert on ultrasound who will look in detail at your baby. This may also happen if the possibility of spina bifida is not excluded by the early blood test which some hospitals offer. In these cases you will normally have a doctor spending at least thirty minutes examining your baby in detail. At the end of this time if he or she tells you that the baby is normal there is only a very small chance of him or her being incorrect.

If there is no reason to suspect that your baby will be abnormal your scan will be performed by a trained ultrasonographer. It should take approximately ten to fifteen minutes and in this time most major abnormalities in your baby will be recognised. It is important, however, to realise that ultrasound can only detect certain types of abnormalities. It will not detect abnormalities caused by genes (e.g. Down's Syndrome). It will show many other abnormalities which cannot be detected by any other means.

No doctor could tell a pregnant woman that she will for certain deliver an entirely normal baby. However, a scan is more likely to indicate any detectable types of abnormality and therefore you can be more reassured by an early scan that your baby will be normal than by any other method of examination.

Will my first Scan tell me if I am having Twins?

Yes. The only accurate way of diagnosing twins in early pregnancy is by scan. If you are having twins they are a little more likely to be small or to be delivered early than if you are only having one baby. In most hospitals you will be offered a monthly scan to ensure that the twins are growing normally.

Are there any other benefits from the first Ultrasound Examination?

Many women enjoy seeing the first visable proof that their baby is a real person especially if it is a first pregnancy. It would be inadvisable to expect to see an instantly recognizable baby on the television screen but you should always ask the ultrasonographer to explain the apparently unidentifiable shapes. Seeing the baby on the screen may overcome many of the worries that you may have had and in many cases it assures you that all is well with the baby.

Who should I take along with me for my first Scan?

I believe that a scan is a family event and therefore encourage both husbands or partners, other children in the family or someone with whom the woman wants to share the experience to be present at the time of the scan. The first scan should be a shared experience and I think that seeing your baby on the screen is part of the family recognition of the pregnancy. In many hospitals, however, it is impractical because of the limited space in the ultrasound department but most hospitals should at least let your husband or partner attend for the examination. Be sure to ask who you can bring when you make your appointment.

Will a Scan help if I bleed or have pain in Early Pregnancy?

Approximately one in four pregnant women will miscarry before twelve weeks. If this is what nature intended there is no way that it can be prevented. In most cases it is easy for the doctor to determine whether you have had a miscarriage by an internal examination. If he or she is unsure and you are more than seven weeks past the first day of your last period it is usually possible to determine by ultrasound if your baby's heart is still beating and for appropriate treatment (usually bed rest) to be started in an attempt to prevent a miscarriage.

Most causes of pain in early pregnancy are harmless and can be readily resolved by your doctor. Certainly ultrasound is not the answer to all complaints and in general you should rely upon your obstetrician to decide whether a scan is indicated or not. For instance if you have had a previous ectopic pregnancy your doctor will undoubtedly order an ultrasound examination at about seven weeks gestation to be sure that this pregnancy is within the womb.

What will happen if the Ultrasonographer does not think that my Baby is Normal?

It is difficult to answer this question as different hospitals have different policies. Ideally the person performing the scan would tell you that they suspect that there is some abnormality in your baby and that they would arrange for a detailed examination to be carried out by a doctor at the same hospital within the next day or two. Following the more detailed ultrasound scan you will be told what was wrong with your baby and the consequences. Any possible treatment would be explained and discussed with you and your husband or partner.

Many hospitals, however, do not have doctors trained to perform such detailed scans and it might be necessary for you to be referred to a large hospital (usually a teaching hospital). This can mean waiting up to about a week before the examination is performed. During the time that you are waiting your obstetrician should see you to try to reassure you until the results of the second scan enable him or her to discuss the abnormalities and their consequences fully.

In some hospitals the person performing the scan is not allowed to tell you if something abnormal is suspected. You will be given a further appointment either at your own hospital or in the teaching hospital within the next week. In such cases you will probably be told that they have been unable to make a particular measurement or that the placenta (afterbirth) is in the wrong place. I do not think that this is the correct way to deal with patients and if this happens I feel that you should insist on seeing your obstetrician and knowing if an abnormality is suspected. I hope that reassurance and a full discussion following the second scan would then follow.

Why should I have a second Scan in the last ten weeks of my Pregnancy?

This scan is to decide if your baby is small and to determine the position of the placenta (afterbirth). If the placenta is found to be low (placenta praevia) you will probably be admitted to hospital. This is a precaution taken because if the placenta covers the cervix (the neck of the womb) you are likely to have very severe bleeding at the time that you have your first contraction and should therefore be under close hospital supervision before your labour starts.

Most second scans show babies of normal size but approximately one in ten, however, will indicate a small baby. Although your obstetrician, midwife or GP will feel the size of the baby at each visit they are only really guessing the size and will miss at least one in three small babies. As with the first scan ultrasound examination is a much more accurate measurement of the size of your baby.

What does it mean if my Baby is Small?

This depends on the type of smallness. Detailed scan measurements are performed on the baby's head and waist to see if the baby is in proportion, in which case it is just a small baby. In such cases no further tests are necessary other than a repeat scan every two weeks to monitor the baby's growth.

If the measurements show that the baby's head is the correct size but the baby's waist is smaller than expected this suggests that the placenta is not providing the baby with adequate nutrition. In addition, as the placenta also provides oxygen to the baby sooner or later your baby will become short of oxygen. In this case you may be admitted to hospital or have detailed tests to confirm that your baby continues in good health depending upon the views of your doctor (see chapter 8 on low birthweight and intrauterine growth retardation). In addition to these tests you will be offered scans every two weeks until you have your baby.

Should I have more than two Scans in my Pregnancy?

In general, if your pregnancy is uncomplicated, two scans are all that is necessary. If, however, you have a complication of pregnancy such as bleeding, high blood pressure or twins, or if you have lost babies in the past you may be offered serial scans. This usually means attending at least every month after your first scan until you deliver your baby. At each attendance the ultrasonographer will measure the size of your baby's head and waist to check that the baby is growing normally. If it is not he/she will tell your doctor who will discuss any problems with you.

Is it possible for the Scan to detect the Sex of my Baby?

This depends upon the skill of the person performing the scan. I never ask women if they want to know the sex of their baby because they may not have given the matter any thought and may later regret knowing in advance. If, however, I am asked what sex the baby is I will do my best to find out. It is never completely foolproof, however, since the only way of telling is by looking between the babies' legs. Obviously if the baby has its legs crossed you cannot see and occasionally mistakes are made because boy babies sometimes hide their penises and a loop of cord may easily be mistaken for a penis in a girl. It is much safer to stifle your curiosity and wait for the surprise at delivery.

What Research is being carried out into Ultrasound?

Continuing research is being carried out into the safety of ultrasound both in the laboratory and by long-term observation studies on children born to mothers who have had ultrasound scans in pregnancy.

Ultrasound is continually being developed and may be used to look at your pregnancy in more detail. The state of health of your baby may be determined by studying both its movements and its breathing movements by means of realtime ultrasound. All fetuses breathe whilst in the uterus and it is thought that these practice breathing movements are necessary for the lungs to develop properly just as movements of the legs appear to be necessary for proper muscle development. Babies who are short of food or oxygen have reduced or absent movements. If you therefore have a fetus that is growing at the less than normal rate your obstetrician may suggest that not only do you keep a record of your baby's movements but that from time to time you have them studied with ultrasound. Recently it has been possible to take blood samples from the umbilical cord by inserting a needle through the womb using ultrasound to guide the point (see chapter 5). In this way a small amount of blood may be collected from the baby to determine if it is receiving sufficient oxygen, or to study its genetic make-up. Indeed this technique has been developed in some hospitals so that should you have a baby that is anaemic because of Rhesus disease it is possible to give the baby repeated transfusions while it is still in the womb.

A new development is the use of Doppler ultrasound to study the pattern of the blood flow both in the umbilical cord and in the blood vessels supplying the placenta. This work is still very much in the realms of a research project but will be offered in some hospitals. It appears that in pre-eclamptic toxaemia of pregnancy (see chapter 7), a condition characterized by high blood pressure, protein in the urine and swelling of the ankles there is often high resistance to the blood flow to the afterbirth. This results in a decreased supply of both food and eventually oxygen to the fetus. There is some suggestion that it may be possible to predict the patients who are going to develop this condition (usually ladies in their first pregnancy) as early as twenty-four weeks by using Doppler ultrasound.

In addition, patients who appear to have small babies on realtime ultrasound may be offered Doppler blood flow studies in later pregnancy. There are many causes for babies being small but the most worrying is when the afterbirth does not supply the baby with adequate food because eventually the afterbirth will also cease to supply the baby with oxygen. By studying the blood flow in the umbilical cord it is possible to tell when the supply of food to the baby has stopped and Doppler studies may also assist in the timing of very small babies. Most small babies, however, do not suffer from this condition (placenta insufficiency) and in these cases the Doppler blood flow studies are normal. This may reassure the obstetrician and allow the patient to be discharged from hospital.

How Safe is my Scan?

Ultrasound scans use high-pitched sound which as it travels

through the body gives energy to the parts of the body. In laboratory conditions this energy has been shown to have some adverse effects. These effects include a rise in temperature within the tissues, abnormal movements of body fluid and tissue cells, abnormal development of cells and possibly the formation of small gas bubbles within tissues. However, in nearly all experiments the amount of ultrasound that has been used is many times greater (at least ten times) than that which is used during your scan. In addition to this your body will rapidly absorb the energy from the scan so that by the time that the ultrasound beam reaches your baby it only contains a fraction of the energy that it started out with.

It is impossible to show that anything is absolutely safe but so far ultrasound scans used in pregnancy have not been shown to have any adverse effects on mothers or babies. Many tests or treatments in medicine are a balance between the good that they do and the harm that they may inflict. In the case of scanning the value of the information gained from the scan for both you and your doctor far outweighs any possible hazards.

7
High Blood Pressure in Pregnancy

Chris Redman

What is Blood Pressure?

The blood circulates around the body driven by the pumping pressure of the heart. This pressure fluctuates up and down with each heart beat, rising to a peak at the end of one beat and sinking to a trough just before the next. Readings of the pressure, therefore, have two parts – 130/80, for example. The 130 is the peak (systolic) and the 80 is the trough (diastolic) pressure.

Just as your pulse (or heart rate) varies from minute to minute, or hour to hour, in response to changing demands in your body, so does your blood pressure. Two readings taken within minutes of each other will be similar but they are unlikely to be the same. Changes of posture, eating, sleeping and taking exercise are some of the activities that will affect it.

Blood pressure can be higher or lower than it should be. If you have ever fainted you will have experienced the effect of an abnormal fall in pressure. Conversely it can be above normal, in which case it is called hypertension. This is a misleading word, wrongly suggesting a state of stress, which leads to the misconception that high blood pressure is something to do with the mental state, and that relaxing, therefore, will reduce the pressure. It is certainly true that some stressful conditions do increase your blood pressure – a full bladder, for example, pain or shortage of sleep – but this is only a small part of the picture. Most of the factors that contribute have no direct link with the mind or emotions.

High blood pressure usually causes no symptoms. The affected person only begins to feel unwell when it enters a short-lived 'malignant' phase, which fortunately is rare. Most people, therefore, have no idea that their pressure is abnormal unless they have it measured. In people who are not pregnant, high blood pressure is important because it wears out the circulation faster. Thus, hardening of the arteries, heart disease and strokes occur more commonly: in women the problem is confined to late middle life and beyond. This is why those who have hypertension need to take treatment indefinitely, to lower the pressure and reduce the wear and tear on the circulation.

Much high blood pressure seems to be inherited. Those who get it are the offspring of a parent or parents who also had it and passed on the relevant genes.

Blood Pressure in Pregnancy

Every aspect of a woman's body changes during pregnancy to meet the needs of her baby, so it is not surprising that her blood pressure should too. What is surprising is that the change is not a rise, but a pronounced fall. Most of the fall will already have occurred by the end of the third month, and the pressure will have reached its lowest point by mid-pregnancy. In the last two or three months it tends to rise, so that at full term it is nearly back to the pre-pregnancy measurement.

Obstetricians and midwives would never need to measure a woman's blood pressure in pregnancy were it not for the complication known as pre-eclampsia, which used to be called toxaemia and causes high blood pressure. To understand the importance of blood pressure in pregnancy it is necessary to understand pre-eclampsia.

What is Pre-Eclampsia?

Pre-eclampsia precedes a very dangerous condition called eclampsia. Fortunately it is now rare, but it can occur at any time in the second half of pregnancy, during labour or in the first days after delivery. Its main feature is the sudden onset of fits or convulsions, similar to epileptic fits. Their onset, without apparent warning, was perplexing until it was discovered that eclampsia is the culmination of a progressive disorder induced by pregnancy, which is now called pre-eclampsia. This can go on for days, weeks or even months, during which time the affected person feels entirely well. There are no symptoms until the final stage, literally hours before the body loses its internal balance and the woman starts to have convulsions. If a woman or her doctors wait until she feels ill before taking action, often it will be too late to ensure her safety. Eclampsia is an extremely dangerous condition for both mother and baby. Even with the best modern care, about one in every ten women who get it before the onset of labour dies. It was a giant step forward, therefore, to be able to recognize pre-eclampsia, even though it manifested no symptoms, and thus to have early warning of a possible catastrophe.

How Pre-Eclampsia is detected

The first warning signal to be discovered was protein in the urine (proteinuria). When the kidneys filter the blood to remove waste products and produce urine, the protein, which is a normal constituent of the blood, is held back because it is needed by the body. However, fairly late in the development of pre-eclampsia, the filters in the kidney become leaky and protein escapes from the blood and appears in the urine.

The second warning signal to be recognized was an increase in the blood pressure. This tends to happen earlier than the leakage of protein into the urine. It is caused by abnormal 'spasm' in the very small arteries throughout the body. Thus the heart has to pump harder to drive the same amount of blood around the system, and the pressure becomes higher.

More recently many other warning signals of pre-eclampsia have been discovered. Most depend on blood tests so that they are not as quick or convenient as those which reveal high blood pressure or proteinuria; but as they have come to light, the true nature of the condition has become clearer, and we are beginning to realize how profound the upsets that it causes are, not only to the blood pressure, but to just about every aspect of the body's functions. It is little wonder that the pre-eclamptic woman becomes so ill.

Why do some women get Pre-Eclampsia?

The condition is extremely common, and suffered to some degree by about one in ten of all pregnant women. The cause of both pre-eclampsia and eclampsia is not known. We know it is inherited, in part, and usually affects women pregnant for the first time. It is thought that the placenta or afterbirth might be responsible. The placenta is the part of the baby (at the end of the umbilical cord) which physically joins him or her to the mother, and provides all the life support (feeding, breathing and so on). For the placenta to do all this successfully it must organize the mother's body to provide all that is needed. In a way it is like the conductor of an orchestra bringing together many different instruments – the different maternal systems – to play one balanced or harmonious tune. The effect of a healthy placenta on a woman's body during a normal pregnancy is extraordinarily potent. It is therefore not hard to appreciate that if the placenta goes wrong, as it does in pre-eclampsia, the tune becomes discordant or even chaotic.

The problem appears to involve the provision of the blood supply from the mother to the placenta. This depends on how well the placenta plants itself in the lining of the womb, which happens in the first four months of pregnancy. If it is poorly established, at some point in the second half of pregnancy it will outgrow its blood supply and the activities of the placenta will become disorganized, and the disturbances we call pre-eclampsia become evident. Thus pre-eclampsia is the final stage of a problem which will have begun long before the diagnosis can be made.

There are two consequences of this picture to consider. The first is that the process of recovery always begins on delivery of the baby, when the sick placenta is removed. Second, high blood pressure is only one of many outward signs of the problem. The high blood pressure is not the cause but simply one consequence of the problem. It does not damage the placenta – something that worries many women who feel guilty that they are in some way responsible for pre-eclampsia. They are not.

The importance of measuring Blood Pressure in Pregnancy

The womb is meant to be a secluded and hidden place for the baby, giving protection from the outside world, which means that the problems of pre-eclampsia that begin in the placenta are hidden and impossible to detect directly. To find out what is happening, doctors and midwives have to look for the outward signs, which are likely to reflect the presence of a sick or struggling placenta. There are many possible disturbances which could be checked, but measuring the blood pressure and checking the urine are the quickest and easiest.

The difficulty is that pre-eclampsia can appear at any time in the second half of pregnancy, can develop very quickly, and can cause no symptoms until it is nearly too late. Therefore the signs must be sought repeatedly in women who themselves feel entirely well. This is the reason behind the repeated checks at antenatal clinics.

What Warning Signals can the mother look for?

This is a treacherous condition and one of its most sinister features is that it is usually not evident to those who have it. About three-quarters of pre-eclamptic women retain too much fluid and become swollen. This is not necessarily a sign, however. Pre-eclampsia can develop without any swelling, and swelling may be no more than a good sign of a healthy pregnancy. Indeed women who have retained some fluid do better than those who have not. The sudden onset of swelling, however, developing over a few days, is not normal, particularly if it involves the *face*. If that happens, a doctor should be consulted immediately.

Other symptoms, but again not exclusive to pre-eclampsia, include headaches, pain in the tummy, vomiting and unclear vision. If these occur it is always essential to have a check-up, although in most instances it will prove to be a false alarm. The check-up should always include a measurement of blood pressure, however, and a urine test for protein.

What can a Pregnant Woman do to help herself?

The successful management of pre-eclampsia depends on three simple but important principles: early diagnosis, early admission to hospital and well-timed delivery. If these are followed, no woman should ever be endangered by the problem.

Early diagnosis
Because pre-eclampsia can develop and progress quickly, it is important not to leave long gaps between check-ups, or early diagnosis will be impossible. More than two weeks is too long, especially after six months. If there are reasons for thinking that the risk is higher than normal then more frequent visits may be needed. No antenatal check-up is ever complete without a blood pressure and urine check. If the doctor or midwife forgets (as

unfortunately can happen) then the expectant mother can help herself by insisting that the checks be done.

Early admission to hospital

The first sign of pre-eclampsia is a rise in the blood pressure. When it is found it is a curious but consistent fact that everyone works hard to discount the finding. The mother will try to explain the high blood pressure away – she feels nervous, she is busy, life is hectic and so on, and all too often the doctor or midwife will yield to these arguments. The correct response, however, is to consider that all rises in the blood pressure are caused by pre-eclampsia until proved otherwise.

This does not mean that you will have to go to hospital immediately, but it does mean that extra care needs to be taken. If the high blood pressure is a one-off, misleading reading, it will soon become apparent. If it is not, then the next step will inevitably be admission to hospital, and if there is definite protein in the urine, then urgent admission is essential because the pre-eclampsia is now well advanced. Women frequently resist, partly because nobody likes hospital, partly because they feel perfectly well, and partly because they have no sense of the dangers of pre-eclampsia. (How many women, after all, know that it is the most important cause of maternal death?) The mother can help herself in all these instances by complying with the medical instructions and not seeking to struggle out of, or break, the safety net that is being put around her.

It is easier to accept admission to hospital if the reason for it is understood. It is not, as is widely understood by the public, midwives, and many doctors, to achieve bed rest. Hospitals are not restful, as anybody who has been in one knows. The true reason is that, beyond a certain stage, pre-eclampsia becomes unpredictable from one day to the next, even from hour to hour in some cases. At one moment all can be well, and at the next a critically dangerous complication can develop. Admission to hospital (a specialist, not a community hospital) places the mother near to help. All is at hand to cope with a sudden crisis, whereas at home the affected individual would be too exposed and vulnerable, unprotected from potentially serious danger.

Obviously when a woman reaches this situation it is better that she can be delivered so that recovery can begin.

Well-timed delivery

Beyond the stage when the woman has both high blood pressure and proteinuria, she must be in hospital and ideally delivered.

This is fine if the pregnancy is sufficiently advanced for the baby to do well, that is at or after about thirty-four to thirty-six weeks. Earlier it may be worthwhile, under the most careful supervision, to remain undelivered to allow the baby to mature some more. However, pre-eclampsia can often be so severe that immediate delivery is essential, regardless of the baby's maturity. In some heartbreaking instances the baby has to be sacrificed to protect the mother's life, but fortunately in the vast majority of cases, the outcome is good for both mother and baby.

Thus by using simple principles of management, the dangers of pre-eclampsia have been all but neutralized. It is one of the unacknowledged triumphs of modern antenatal care.

Prevention

The situation would be better still if the condition could be prevented entirely, but because the cause of pre-eclampsia is not understood, specific preventive treatment is not available. Instead there are a number of recommendations arising from various people's theories. Pre-eclampsia is called the disease of theories. Most are unhelpful.

Bed rest
Once pre-eclampsia begins, it progresses despite strictly enforced bed rest. There is no convincing evidence that bed rest makes the problem easier, although lying down definitely makes the blood pressure lower. This is true of everybody, whether pregnant or not, and reflects the body's control systems in different positions. As already mentioned, the level of the blood pressure is merely the reflection of the internal problems affecting the placenta. By making the blood pressure appear to be lower, no substantial alteration in the underlying disease process has been achieved. As discussed, the need to be admitted to hospital is not to enforce bed rest, but to place the affected woman near to help should she suddenly need it.

Diet
Pre-eclampsia runs in families (i.e. it is genetic); it affects women having their first babies, and is not related to social class. Thus the pattern of its occurrence is not obviously related to dietary habits. There may be factors in the diet which are important, but claims that a particular diet, on its own, can solve the problem,

are spurious. In general, of course, it is important that all pregnant women eat a good, well-balanced diet (see Chapter 1).

Weight restriction
The belief that plump women are particularly susceptible to pre-eclampsia is now known to be wrong. Furthermore, the excessive weight gain that occurs in some cases is not caused by over-eating, but by abnormal fluid retention. This cannot be controlled by dieting. The belief that it is merely necessary to restrict weight gain by a certain amount to guarantee protection from pre-eclampsia is incorrect.

Salt restriction
For non-pregnant people with mildly raised blood pressure, salt restriction is sensible. In pregnancy it is not. The only major study that has been conducted showed that those who restricted their use of salt suffered more pre-eclampsia and more often lost their babies.

Sedatives
These are still used in the belief that sedation controls the blood pressure and lessens the chance of fits, but there is no place for sedatives in the management of pre-eclampsia. They do not control the blood pressure and should not be used for this purpose. Some, but not all, do help prevent fits, but they are not the only drugs that do. If there is a risk of convulsion the first priority is to administer not a sedative but an anti-convulsant drug (see below).

Blood pressure drugs
Since high blood pressure is not the cause of pre-eclampsia its control does not prevent the problem. However, in certain circumstances blood pressure drugs must be used because very high blood pressure is, of itself, dangerous. The drugs are used solely to protect the mother. A number are available and in general it is known that they do not upset the baby.

Anti-convulsant drugs
These are used when fits are thought to be imminent. The drugs used in the United Kingdom happen to be strong sedatives as well, so that those who experience the treatment have confused memories of what happened. If fits are thought to be likely then delivery must be organized immediately, and because the risk of fits persists for a while after delivery, the treatment needs to be continued for a day or so.

What is the effect of Pre-Eclampsia on the Baby?

The baby is nearly always affected by trouble in the placenta. He or she may become under-nourished ('small-for-dates') because the feeding functions of the placenta are less than they should be. Alternatively, if the breathing functions are affected the baby may begin to suffocate, and in extreme cases may die of suffocation. So he or she needs to be monitored carefully before and during labour. Sometimes the problems are so severe that the baby would not survive labour, in which case a Caesarean section must be done.

Will it recur with a subsequent Pregnancy?

This is the first question of anyone who has suffered severe pre-eclampsia, usually in the first pregnancy. The answer is that the majority will not. About one in ten or twenty will, although usually less severely the second time. A small number of women get it with every pregnancy, sometimes more severely with each one. This is more likely to happen in those who already have medical disorders such as particular kidney diseases. Not many women who have already had uncomplicated pregnancies start suffering pre-eclampsia with their second or third, but it can happen.

Does Pre-Eclampsia affect health in the long-term?

Normally not. The vast majority of women who have suffered pre-eclampsia can expect to recover fully and their health remains unaffected in the long term. In extremely rare circumstances, however, it can cause irreversible catastrophes. In some women the condition brings to light a medical problem which has been there all the time, but gone unnoticed. In these cases, although the pre-eclampsia at first sight appears to have caused the problem, it is in fact merely the reason for its discovery. In these cases the women's future health depends on the nature of the problem that has been revealed.

The Importance of Chronic Hypertension

Some women already have high blood pressure before they

conceive for the first time, and the question arises as to how this can affect the pregnancy. These women are more susceptible to pre-eclampsia, but even so, the majority do not get it and their pregnancies progress normally despite their high blood pressure. Some are already taking treatment for their blood pressure and most of the drugs used appear to be safe even if taken for the full nine months. Some, however, used less commonly for more severe hypertension are probably not safe for the baby. So it is wise to discuss these issues with the doctor in advance.

Because normal pregnancy lowers the blood pressure, many women who are hypertensive beforehand have normal blood pressures by the time they have reached the end of the first three months, thus the need for treatment temporarily disappears. This happy state of affairs begins to change in the final three months, however, and treatment usually has to be resumed, quite safely, at this point. None of the commonly used drugs need interfere with breast feeding.

Summary

High blood pressure is one of the many signs of pre-eclampsia. The condition itself appears to be caused by the placenta and inevitably affects the baby's safety. It cannot be prevented, but is 'cured' by delivery, that is, by removing the placenta. We cope with this dangerous, common and unpredictable disorder is by keeping one step ahead of events. Because pre-eclampsia causes no symptoms, the first warning of its presence is a rise in blood pressure, and later protein in the urine. Therefore it is vitally important that these should be measured at every antenatal check-up.

8

Intrauterine Growth Retardation

Philip J. Steer

What is Intrauterine Growth Retardation?

Strictly speaking, babies should only be called growth retarded when they have grown to a smaller size than they were intended to be on the basis of their genetic programming. All of us carry such genes in our chromosomes which are the 'blueprints' resident in the nucleus (centre) of nearly every cell in our body. A distinction needs to be made here between the genes which regulate weight at birth and those which govern the eventual size of the adult. Birth weight depends upon a complex interaction between baby and mother, and thus the weight of the mother has ten times more influence than the weight of the father on the birthweight of the baby; the eventual adult weight is determined fifty/fifty by the mother and father.

It is not possible to read the genes to know what the birthweight of the baby should be, so that we have to decide whether a baby is growth retarded on various indirect criteria. One way to get an idea is to work out where a baby falls in relation to all the other babies of the same sex (birthweight is higher in males than in females) and of the same gestational age (babies born prematurely are obviously smaller than those born at term). Large studies have been carried out to determine the normal distribution of birthweight and those that fall below the tenth centile (i.e. only ten per cent of babies of the same age are smaller than this value) are labelled as 'small for gestational age' (SGA). These babies are often labelled as suffering from 'intrauterine growth retardation' (IUGR) but in fact probably about two-thirds of them are actually quite normal and are simply genetically small individuals.

How then do we tell which of these small babies are genuinely growth retarded and which are small but normal? Making the distinction depends on appreciating a further subdivision of small babies, those with symmetrical and those with asymmetrical growth retardation.

Symmetrically growth retarded babies, which account for about half of the growth retarded babies born, are apparently normally formed but have fewer cells in their body than their normal peers. Such growth retardation is usually due to some insult to the fetus early in pregnancy which has interfered with the replication of the body's cells. This could be an infection, such as rubella (German measles) or cytomegalovirus or exposure to chemicals (such as nicotine or excessive amounts of caffeine). Another important cause of symmetrical growth retardation is abnormality of the chromosomes such as Down's Syndrome. Unfortunately the long term prognosis for these babies is often poor since the damage is deep seated and cannot be corrected by later management either in utero or after birth.

Asymmetrical growth retardation is due to an influence later in pregnancy interfering with the energy supply to the fetus. This gives rise to a baby which is 'starved'. It cannot lay down proper fat reserves under its skin, or glycogen (another energy storage compound) in its liver. Because of this the baby's body is small, but fortunately the brain is the last organ to be affected in the process and so the head of these babies appears larger than the body (hence the 'asymmetrical' part of the description). Such babies tend to suffer 'distress' in labour (especially if the oxygen supply via the placenta is compromised). After birth they are often hypoglycaemic (low blood sugar) and become cold very easily. They also tend to suck poorly because they lack the energy stores for vigorous feeding. However, because the brain is relatively unaffected, the long-term outlook for these babies is very good provided they are cared for properly in labour and after birth. Conditions commonly associated with asymmetrical growth retardation include pre-eclampsia and maternal underweight.

How can we recognize Growth Retardation before Birth?

A number of factors in the mother's history can alert us to the possibility that she might have a growth retarded baby. A previously affected baby means that there is about a thirty per cent chance of a subsequent baby being SGA. Chronic severely high blood pressure is another predisposing factor, and there are a number of rare medical conditions (such as lupus erythematosus) which are also important predictors. More commonly, heavy smoking is a risk factor. Women who are underweight (previous anorexics for example) also have a high risk of producing an SGA baby, as do older women (who are more likely to have a Down's infant, for example). Other signs can be detected at the antenatal booking clinic. Women who respond well to pregnancy show a marked increase in the fluid component of their blood which causes their haemoglobin (Hb) concentration to fall from the normal non-pregnant level of about 14 g/dl to about 10–12 g/dl. At one time this was wrongly thought to represent anaemia, but now we know it is a good sign. Women who do not show this drop have an increased chance of developing high blood pressure and having small babies (although of course some women do become genuinely anaemic during pregnancy and values of Hb less than 9.5 g/dl are also associated with growth retardation). Other normal symptoms of pregnancy such as nausea, tiredness and ankle swelling (oedema) are also associated with a good outcome, and if a woman fails to show these at all the obstetrician or midwife should be more vigilant than average. A high alphafetoprotein (AFP) level in the blood (used as a screen for anencephaly and spina bifida) is also associated with a higher risk of growth retardation.

A number of observations in the antenatal period can also alert the obstetrician or midwife. Women of low or normal body weight who fail to gain the normal amount of weight over the pregnancy (about 10–15 kg) are more at risk of IUGR. Small fluctuations in weight from week to week should not cause alarm since they often reflect simply how much water has been drunk that day (or lost if the weather is hot!). Obese women (more than twenty per cent over the ideal body weight) seem to be able to grow their babies normally even if they do not gain weight (presumably using their stored energy) and lack of weight gain in such women is therefore not of any significance – indeed it should probably be encouraged since they have an increased chance of having very large babies which can become stuck during birth ('shoulder dystocia'). Fat women can however have growth retarded babies for other reasons, such as high blood pressure.

The simplest method of assessing the fetus's growth is 'fundal height measurement'. The obstetrician or midwife uses a tape measure to assess the distance from the symphysis pubis (pubic bone) to the fundus (top of the uterus). This method cannot be used until about eighteen weeks gestation, since before then the majority of the baby is in the pelvis, but, after this, the symphysis-fundal height measured in centimetres approximately equals the gestational period in weeks up until about thirty-four weeks. After thirty-four weeks, the baby grows more slowly and the volume of amniotic fluid around the baby decreases, so that the symphysis-fundal height may not increase much. If the symphysis-fundal height is more than four centimetres less than the gestational age at any stage, the baby may be growth retarded and further investigation is indicated. It should be borne in mind, however, that it is not only the size of the baby that influences the symphysis-fundal height. In fat women for example it may appear to be as much as 8 cm larger due to her fat layer adding to the babies' apparent size. In contrast, tall women often 'hide' more of the baby in their pelvis so that the symphysis-fundal height appears less than normal. Careful use of this technique can pick up about sixty to seventy per cent of IUGR babies.

If growth retardation is suspected, either from risk factors or clinical signs, such as a reduced symphysis-fundal height measurement, further tests are usually indicated. The most useful of these is ultrasound scanning. These days most women have a routine scan at about eighteen weeks to check for fetal abnormalities. Since it is unusual for a baby to be severely growth retarded at eighteen weeks, the finding of a small baby at this stage suggests that the dates of the last menstrual period were misleading, and the baby is 'younger' than previously thought. Scans subsequent to eighteen weeks can therefore be plotted with confidence at the right gestation on a chart which indicates the size the baby ought to be at any given stage of pregnancy (there is of course a range of normal which increases with advancing gestation). If the baby is smaller than it ought to be then we know that the baby is 'small for dates'. A number of different measurements are made to guard against mistakes, and also to tell if the growth retardation is symmetrical (normal ratio of head to body) or asymmetrical. Common measurements include biparietal diameter (width of the head from side to side), head circumference, abdominal circumference and femur (upper leg bone) length. Measurement of the amount of amniotic fluid is also useful, as growth retardation is often associated with reduced amounts (oligohydramnios).

A new ultrasound test which is gradually becoming more

widely available, and which holds promise, is the measurement of the rate with which the blood flows through the uterine, placental and fetal blood vessels. This is done with 'Doppler ultrasound' (see chapter 5) and produces readings correctly termed 'blood velocity waveforms' although often incorrectly referred to as 'blood flow'. These measurements are particularly valuable if IUGR is due to high blood pressure or other conditions which are associated with a reduced blood supply to the placenta (we think that in many cases it is the reduced blood flow which causes the mother to increase her blood pressure to try and correct the deficit). On the other hand the measurement of blood velocity is not so helpful if the IUGR is due to other factors, for example if the baby is genetically abnormal or if the mother is malnourished (poor food supply), because in these cases the velocity waveform is usually normal.

If there is a suspicion that the baby is abnormal (for example cleft lip, failure to detect the kidneys, reduced or excessive amniotic fluid) then a needle can be passed under ultrasound control into the umbilical vein to sample the baby's blood (a technique called 'cordocentesis') (see chapter 6). The blood can be analyzed to check that the baby's chromosomes are normal, and if not, termination of pregnancy may be appropriate. This technique can also be used later in pregnancy to measure the oxygen level and acidity of the baby's blood.

Chemicals produced from the placenta (for example human placental lactogen, HPL) or placenta and fetus (for example oestriol, E3) can also be measured in a maternal blood sample as an index of size and function: high levels mean that a growth retarded baby is unlikely. However, they are not very sensitive and these days are used less and less. They are sometimes used as a screening test when an ultrasound may not be available or may be inconvenient.

How do we manage a Baby with IUGR?

At the present time there are very few useful treatments for growth retardation. Fetal abnormality for example is not usually amenable to correction. Oxygen given to the mother has shown some promise in a small group with poor placental blood flow but this requires monitoring with cordocentesis and is not yet widely available.

Management therefore depends heavily on monitoring the growth and well-being of the fetus, and delivering the baby if it stops growing altogether or if it shows signs of oxygen shortage. The latter is usually screened for by regular monitoring of the fetal heart rate using a cardiotocograph machine. The heart rate is measured for about half an hour at a time. The normal heart rate pattern has a baseline rate of between 120 and 160 beats per minute, and fluctuates by about five beats per minute every minute (the fluctuation is called variability). Sudden increases in rate (accelerations) are also a healthy sign. The heart rate should not exhibit slowings (decelerations) with Braxton-Hicks contractions. Thus, loss of variability, lack of accelerations (a 'non-reactive' tracing) and the presence of decelerations are all indications that urgent delivery should be considered. These days neonatal care is so good that elective delivery can be entertained from as early as twenty-six weeks when survival rate is about sixty per cent; by thirty weeks the survival rate exceeds ninety-five per cent. Early in pregnancy delivery is often by caesarean section to avoid further stress on the baby and because the cervix is not usually 'ripe' (soft and dilated) enough to allow induction of labour. After about thirty-four weeks however, if the cervix is favourable, induction of labour is often attempted because, perhaps surprisingly, about sixty per cent of growth retarded babies will tolerate labour safely.

An important thing the mother can do herself is to monitor the baby's activity – the so-called 'kick count'. If a baby moves more than ten times from nine a.m. to nine p.m. then it is unlikely to be in serious trouble. Sudden reductions or indeed cessation of fetal movements should always be reported to the obstetrician or midwife straight away – don't wait until the next day when it may be too late! The mother should also of course pay careful attention to her diet and if she is a smoker should make an especial attempt to give up.

Bed rest for the mother is often recommended if her baby is not growing, but the evidence that bed rest is valuable is not strong. This, together with the reduction in hospital beds which has been a feature of the last ten years, has generated a trend to 'outpatient monitoring', sometimes in an 'antenatal day care' ward.

These days most growth retarded babies that are detected in utero can be delivered in good shape and will subsequently do well, many exhibiting 'catch-up' growth. Future progress will be made by diagnosing more and more accurately the cause of the growth retardation in each individual case, and developing specific therapies aimed primarily at prevention of the many and varied conditions which cause it.

9

Diabetes in Pregnancy

Michael Maresh

Many pregnant women who are not diabetics, are told that they might have diabetes associated with their pregnancy. The following introduction, together with a section on this form of pregnancy associated diabetes, should clarify the situation for them. For those who have diabetes outside pregnancy, the section on insulin dependent diabetes will enable them to understand more about the management of their pregnancy.

Diabetes occurs when there is not enough insulin being produced by the pancreas to meet the body's needs. The pancreas lies behind the stomach and makes chemicals, some of which are released into the gut to help with food digestion, and others, such as insulin, which pass straight into the bloodstream. Insulin is crucial in keeping the levels of glucose in our blood as near constant as possible despite our irregular food intake, and is at the centre of many internal processes; without it we cannot survive.

In the non-pregnant state there are broadly speaking two forms of diabetes.

1. Insulin dependent diabetes. This is caused by a failure of the pancreas so that it produces hardly any or no insulin and if the patient is not given insulin she would become very ill.

2. Non-insulin dependent diabetes. This is found in people who do not produce enough insulin for their requirements and tend to have higher blood glucose than normal. They are often overweight and a reduction in weight may allow the insulin they produce to be used more efficiently. In addition, by avoiding foods from which glucose is rapidly absorbed into the bloodstream (e.g. sweets, cakes) they can often obtain normal glucose levels throughout the day without the need for drugs. There are

cases, however, when drugs are needed to help the body use its natural insulin more efficiently; but treatment with insulin injections is only rarely used in this type of diabetic. Insulin dependent diabetics also have to be careful about their weight and diet, or they will constantly have to alter their insulin dosages to achieve normal blood glucose levels.

Normal pregnancy is sometimes referred to as being diabetogenic because it can trigger diabetes. Many changes occur in the way the body works at this time, all no doubt for the benefit of the fetus. What occurs with regard to insulin and the pancreas is that the body cannot use its natural insulin as efficiently as before and the pancreas responds by producing more insulin. Thus in normal pregnancy after a meal the glucose levels will be initially higher, but the extra insulin will eventually clear the glucose from the blood so that before the next meal the blood glucose levels are normal. Some women, however, particularly if they are obese, don't adapt sufficiently and their insulin doesn't produce much of an effect. This results in their blood glucose levels being higher than normal for most of the day. These women are often called 'gestational diabetics' (see below). This form of diabetes can also arise if the pancreas cannot produce enough insulin to meet the additional amount required in pregnancy, with the result that the blood glucose levels are again higher than normal.

The insulin dependent woman suffers from the same problem during pregnancy. The body's use of insulin becomes increasingly inefficient so that more and more insulin needs to be injected to keep blood glucose levels at normal concentrations. Since these two problems of gestational diabetes and insulin dependent diabetes apply to different groups of women they are discussed in detail in separate sections, although there are similarities in management.

Insulin Dependent Diabetes

Before the advent of insulin treatment, pregnancy was a hazardous condition for the diabetic. Insulin made it considerably safer, but maternal and fetal losses still remained high and it is only today that large centres report figures comparable to those for normal pregnant women. What we have come to realize is that if diabetes is very tightly controlled during pregnancy, so that blood glucose levels are within normal pregnancy range (glucose levels are expressed in terms of mmol per litre (mmol/l) and are normally less than 7 mmol/l, except after meals), then there is less need for obstetric intervention, such as early delivery, and the pregnancy should be able to continue normally. Tight control, however, can be very hard to achieve and demands a lot from the woman, her family and those looking after her. Some diabetics may find it impossible and if so they must not feel that they have failed; but they should continue to aim for perfection for the sake of the successful outcome of their pregnancy.

It is important that tight diabetic control starts before conception, as this may decrease both the risk of miscarriage, and of the fetus developing abnormally. Most women are not seen until seven to eight weeks after their last menstrual period, however, by which time most of the major structures of the fetus have already been formed, so a diabetic woman wishing to conceive should try to ensure her control is good before she stops using contraceptives and should therefore consult her doctor.

The woman also needs to decide where to have her baby, whether to go to the nearest maternity unit or to be referred to a more central unit, often a teaching hospital. There are naturally arguments both ways. To go to the nearest hospital will be easier logistically for her and also easier for family and visitors should she have to spend time in hospital during her pregnancy. On the other hand, the average obstetrician will only look after about two diabetic mothers a year and therefore it may be harder for him to give the detailed, individualized care required for each mother. There are four key people involved in the mother's care in pregnancy; the obstetrician, physician, dietitian and midwife. All are indispensable and it is of crucial importance that all can communicate easily whenever the woman attends. This has led to combined clinics being set up in many of the larger teaching units and in a number of local district hospitals with all diabetics being transferred to the care of one obstetrician. These clinics look after eight to thirty women each year, which enables them to become very experienced, to distinguish more easily between the problems, and to adopt a more individual approach. It also makes it easier for diabetic women to discuss their pregnancy problems together. Another advantage of going to a central unit is that an intensive care neonatal unit will be routinely available. Despite advances, some mothers still have to be delivered early, especially if they have diabetic complications.

Ideally a diabetic should consider these issues prior to pregnancy and discuss them with her general practitioner who should be able to find out, if he does not already know, the services available in the region for management of diabetic pregnancy. If she should decide to attend a hospital for her pregnancy she has not been to before, then a pre-pregnancy consultation is advisable. Apart from discussions about how the pregnancy will be managed, the consultant may decide to alter her insulin regime in preparation for the type she will be on in pregnancy.

Even though the diabetes may have been well controlled prior to conception it can be disrupted very early on in pregnancy. This is because the placenta produces chemicals which make the insulin action less efficient. In addition, there may be a change in food intake because of the nausea and vomiting common in early pregnancy. Accordingly, once pregnancy is suspected an urgent hospital appointment should be made. For the woman already under the hospital where she proposes to deliver a telephone call to the diabetic physician's secretary or, if there is a combined clinic, to the consultant obstetrician's secretary should ensure an appointment within a week. A referral letter from her GP can follow. For a woman not under the hospital where she plans to deliver, her GP will normally ring through to fix an urgent appointment and not wait for potential delays with a routine letter.

As already mentioned, there is a need for more insulin to be given as pregnancy advances. If good control is lost, even for a short period, it can have an adverse effect on the fetus (see below), so there is some urgency in achieving normal glucose levels. In the past this has meant regular hospital admissions, particularly in the last few months of pregnancy, to adjust insulin dosages to improve control. However, more recently it has become possible to monitor glucose concentrations at home. A drop of blood, obtained by pricking a finger, is put on a sensitive reagent strip. This can be read with the naked eye or with the use of a portable meter (generally available at about £75) and has meant that patients can make regular insulin adjustments quite safely on an outpatient basis. As well as changing the dosage, it may be necessary to alter the schedule by giving additional short-acting insulin before the midday meal in order to achieve good control throughout the twenty-four hours.

Hospital admissions have thereby been dramatically cut, although clearly they may be needed from time to time if the patient is not managing to achieve good control as an out-patient. The decrease in physical activity in hospital, however, can lead to too much insulin being given, so that when the woman goes home she may have a tendency to low glucose concentrations and subsequent hypoglycaemic attacks ('hypos'). These attacks are very worrying for the diabetic and her family, but there is no evidence to suggest that they harm the fetus.

Of much more concern to the fetus is if the mother does not

receive enough insulin. Excessive amounts of glucose, fats and amino acids can then cross to the fetus. The fetal pancreas responds to this particularly after about the twenty-sixth week of pregnancy by producing extra insulin which promotes excessive growth in the fetus, and may also temporarily effect other organs such as the bone marrow and lungs. Excessive amniotic fluid (the fluid surrounding the fetus) may also develop under these conditions. A regular examination of the mother's abdomen, therefore, will give the obstetrician a marker of how good the diabetic control is, as will regular ultrasound measurements of the fetus and assessment of the amniotic fluid volume. It is when things are not going smoothly that the combined clinic approach is so crucial.

It is often claimed that diabetics run a higher risk of having complications in their pregnancies, such as blood pressure problems or premature labour. However, if the diabetes can be well controlled then there is no more risk of these problems developing than in non-diabetics.

In the recent past obstetricians often delivered diabetics at about thirty-six weeks' gestation. This arose because of the occasional inexplicable death of a normal fetus at this stage of pregnancy and also because of the desire to deliver the baby before it became too big.

With hindsight these losses were probably associated with poor diabetic control. Delivering early brought its problems; the mother suffered a high Caesarean section rate; and the babies often had significant (even though transient) breathing problems associated with slight prematurity, delivery by Caesarean section, and imperfectly controlled diabetes. Accordingly, there has been an increasing trend to allow well-controlled diabetics to go to full term, hoping for a spontaneous onset of labour and thus a higher chance of normal delivery. This in turn makes it less likely that the babies will need to be observed on the special baby unit, but will be able to go straight to the postnatal ward. While becoming more flexible in their approach to diabetics, obstetricians have tended to use additional methods such as fetal movement counting and antenatal heart rate monitoring to assess fetal well-being. Nevertheless, it may well be necessary in the diabetic who is difficult to control or who has complications, such as protein in the urine, to deliver them at thirty-seven to thirty-eight weeks. If the clinical and ultrasound judgement is that the baby is very big a Caesarean is often advised to avoid possible damage to the baby during delivery; otherwise labour will be induced. If it seems likely that the baby is to go to the special care unit then a visit beforehand is advisable for the mother to set her mind at rest.

Management in labour is only complicated by the fact that once it is established the woman should not eat; unless labour is very rapid she will usually be given insulin and glucose via an intravenous drip. Various regimes are used, such as giving the insulin intravenously by a continuous pump. If the woman has a glucose meter it may be helpful for her to have it with her so that she and her partner can do regular checks during labour, to supplement those which may be sent to the laboratory. Provided that there are no problems with glucose control there is no reason why labour cannot proceed normally and no arbitrary time limit need be set just because the mother is diabetic.

After delivery the baby will have regular heel pricks to check its blood glucose. If its pancreas had been overstimulated in late pregnancy by the mother's glucose levels being a little high, then it will be producing extra insulin temporarily and so it may develop low glucose levels until feeding is well established. Newborn babies normally have low glucose levels (down to about 2mmol/l) and the mother should not be worried by this.

The mother now has to reduce her insulin to a level similar to that she had before pregnancy. She can afford to relax her tight control slightly while she establishes her lactation and new routines. There is absolutely no reason why a diabetic cannot breastfeed although she may need to increase her dietary intake. Pregnancy is often very rewarding for a diabetic in that it can give her more insight into the degree of control she can achieve.

Finally there is the question of contraception. Although there were claims that the intrauterine contraceptive device had a high failure rate in diabetic women, this has not been substantiated and so can still be recommended. Most physicians are not keen on diabetics taking the combined oral contraceptive pill for long periods since both diabetes and the Pill are associated with an increased risk of vascular disease. No such stigma holds for the 'progesterone only pill'. Finally, of course, barrier methods are medically if not aesthetically the ideal. Although there is no evidence to suggest that diabetes deteriorates during pregnancy, the tight control needed to achieve a normal pregnancy outcome may not be easy with a number of children and there is a tendency for diabetic mothers to request sterilization after two or three children.

Gestational Diabetes

There has been concern over the last forty years that there are pregnant women who unknowingly have or will shortly develop non-insulin dependent diabetes. It is because insulin action is not so efficient in pregnancy that this milder form of diabetes could deteriorate and adversely affect the fetus in ways that can occur with insulin dependent diabetes. In addition, there are women, often overweight, who have an exaggerated pregnancy response to the handling of insulin (see p. 69) so that insulin action becomes very inefficient. These women may, just during pregnancy, have higher than normal glucose concentrations which could affect the fetus. This is strictly speaking the classic 'gestational diabetes', the abnormality only being present in pregnancy. During pregnancy, however, it is usually impossible to distinguish these types of diabetes and it is not necessary to do so at this stage; what matters for the fetus is the levels of glucose in the mother's blood. Here the term gestational diabetes will be used for all women with abnormal glucose concentrations in pregnancy, who are not insulin dependent diabetics.

Obstetricians have looked for ways of detecting women who unknowingly have high glucose levels. This is the reason behind the routine testing of urine at the antenatal clinic for glucose in the urine (glycosuria). However, in most pregnant women glycosuria does not occur unless the blood glucose concentration is greater than 10mmol/l, which is unusual in normal pregnancy. A woman could regularly have a blood concentration of about eight and only occasionally go above ten, thus rarely having glycosuria. Yet this high glucose concentration could result in the problems met by the insulin dependent diabetic. Thus glycosuria is not sensitive enough, only detecting abnormalities when they are severe. Also, some pregnant women have glycosuria at normal blood levels, causing unnecessary worry.

The definitive test as to whether there is an abnormality is to do a glucose tolerance test. This assesses how the body can handle a large amount of glucose. A measured amount of glucose is swallowed (either 50 or 75 grams) and to ensure standard results nothing should be eaten beforehand – an overnight fast is the most practical method. Blood samples are taken before the glucose is given and then half hourly for two to three hours to measure the glucose concentrations in the blood. Unfortunately, there is not universal agreement as to the upper limits of normal. It is not feasible to perform a glucose tolerance test on all pregnant women; many obstetricians reserve it for women who are more likely to be at risk, that is those with so-called 'potential diabetic' features. These are: having glycosuria; being overweight; having a close relative with diabetes; having lost a baby in the past for no obvious reason; having previously had an abnormal glucose tolerance test; and having previously had a large baby. Not all women with abnormal glucose tolerance are 'potential diabetics' and so some obstetricians have looked at other methods of screening. They take blood samples for glucose measurement either randomly or after a glucose drink at an antenatal clinic visit when blood needs to be taken for other reasons. If the glucose concentration is high then the full glucose tolerance test needs to be performed.

The reason why screening for gestational diabetes is not universally practised is that its relevance remains controversial. Mothers with gestational diabetes tend to have heavier babies, but to a large extent this can be accounted for by these mothers being more likely to be overweight (which is associated with bigger babies) rather than by them having raised glucose concentrations. Other problems classically associated with the newborn of the insulin dependent diabetic, such as transient low glucose levels, do occur in gestational diabetes, but usually only in those with the more marked glucose abnormalities. Although the exact degree of glucose abnormality which is significant is controversial, current opinion is that if the mother persistently has a high glucose concentration in the blood before meals (more than 6mmol/l) then she should be given insulin injections for the duration of the pregnancy. This insulin treatment needs to be supplemented by changes in diet whereby the mother avoids the rapidly absorbed carbohydrate foods (e.g. cakes, sweets) and decreases her total calorie intake. If the mother has normal glucose levels in her blood before meals and just abnormally high ones afterwards this type of dietary modification alone should suffice.

Other aspects of management will also depend on the severity of the glucose abnormality. If insulin is required regular attention to blood glucose concentrations are necessary up until delivery, just as with the insulin dependent diabetic. Similarly careful attention to the rate of growth of the fetus will also indicate whether the diabetic control is good enough. Induction of labour is not often performed for those just being treated by diet, but may well be required for those who have needed insulin therapy for the same reasons as in the insulin dependent diabetic, such as excessive fetal growth. For this reason most gestational diabetics have regular ultrasound in the latter part of pregnancy as an additional safeguard. In labour insulin therapy is usually not required, but blood glucose concentrations will be checked and if they are high and labour is prolonged, insulin may be given. After delivery, all insulin therapy is stopped since, with the placenta delivered, the pregnancy adaptations stop and the mother rapidly reverts to her pre-pregnancy insulin/glucose state. Blood glucose measurements will usually be made to check that this has occurred. The baby will have blood taken from a heel prick to ensure it does not have low glucose levels (see above).

It is important for the mother that she returns for a glucose tolerance test a few months after delivery. If this remains abnormal then she will be referred to a diabetic clinic where it can be decided whether she needs just dietary advice or tablets as well. If the test is normal it is important that she does not become overweight or, if she is, that she reduces to her ideal weight. There is no doubt that in the long term she is more at risk of developing non-insulin dependent diabetes than the general population. However, by keeping to her ideal weight she can dramatically decrease this risk. If she becomes pregnant again then the glucose tolerance test is again likely to become abnormal, but whether the problem will be more or less severe is difficult to predict. There is often reluctance to prescribe the combined oral contraceptive pill, because it may worsen the glucose handling by the body. In fact, the modern low dosage pills appear to have a neglible effect on this, but there may be other reasons for not prescribing it, such as being older or overweight. There are no particular reasons why any of the other contraceptive methods cannot be used.

10
Monitoring in Labour

Naren Patel

Nowadays the commonly used phrase 'monitoring in labour' normally applies to the electronic recording of the fetal heart rate and uterine contractions, both of which provide vital information about how well the baby is bearing up to the strain of labour.

Doctors first began listening to the fetal heart in the early nineteenth century, initially as a means of ascertaining that the baby was alive. It was later noted that the heart beat slowed down during uterine contractions, and further research into the changes in the baby's heart rate during labour brought about the term 'fetal distress', which is used today.

Fetal Distress

Normally the baby derives his or her oxygen supply from the mother's blood via the placental blood vessels. Every time a uterine contraction occurs the blood vessels of the uterus are constricted, and thus the supply of oxygenated blood to the baby can be temporarily reduced. Healthy babies are not at all affected by this because they have enough in reserve, and once the contraction has passed and the oxygen supply improves, they recover quickly. It is rather like holding one's breath moment-arily. If, however, the oxygen supply is further reduced, or the baby has less in reserve, it can have a damaging effect. Any change in the fetal heart rate, therefore, can indicate a change in the oxygen supply and we can thus diagnose 'lack of oxygen'.

Electronic Fetal Monitoring

In the past, doctors and nurses recorded the baby's heart rate by listening through a small stethoscope placed on the mother's abdomen. This had its limitations, because in labour it could only be done at regular intervals, and the heart beat was often difficult to hear during contractions. As a result a significant percentage of babies suffering from lack of oxygen were missed, while many cases of 'fetal distress' were erroneously diagnosed in situations which were not life-threatening to the baby.

In the late 1960s machines were developed which made continuous monitoring of the fetal heart rate and uterine contractions possible. This has reduced unnecessary interference in healthy babies and enabled doctors to identify earlier those babies who may be suffering from a reduction in their oxygen

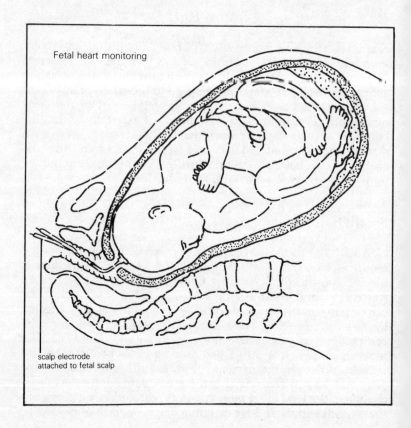

Fetal heart monitoring

scalp electrode
attached to fetal scalp

supply. If this is picked up early enough appropriate steps can be taken, such as obtaining a sample of blood from the baby's scalp, or delivering the baby, before there is any likelihood of long term damage.

The fetal heart rate is recorded either 'externally', using an ultrasound monitor strapped on to the mother's abdomen, or 'internally', via a small electrode attached to the baby's scalp (Fig 1). These devices are connected to a machine which converts the heart beat to heart rate per minute, and prints it out on paper.

Since it is changes in the fetal heart rate that occur during and after uterine contractions that are important in the diagnosis of fetal distress, the contractions must also be recorded. This is normally done by strapping a small disc to the mother's abdomen or, occasionally, by placing a catheter (small hollow tube) or a recording device into the uterus. These record pressure changes which are then printed out by the machine on to the paper.

The normal fetal heart rate lies between 120 and 160 beats per minute in a baby at term. During contractions there are small variations in the rate, either in the form of increase or decrease. Any abnormal variation alerts midwives and doctors early, and if there is any doubt about the ability of the fetus to withstand the stress of labour, or if the changes in the fetal heart rate are suspicious, then a small specimen of blood will be taken by making a superficial puncture in the baby's scalp. This is a very simple procedure, which only takes a few minutes and causes no pain or damage to the baby. The blood is then analysed immediately in the labour room, and its acidity checked to assess the amount of oxygen it contains. This is called 'fetal blood sampling'.

Drawbacks

Like all medical tests, fetal monitoring is not perfect and there are drawbacks. Accurate recording, when carried out externally, is dependent on the ultrasound probe being located properly, and the fetal movement or positional change can affect this. If the monitoring is being done internally, the scalp electrode needs to be properly attached to the baby's scalp.

Occasionally there may be problems with machines malfunctioning; and interpretation of the print-out can be difficult, particularly if there is electrical interference. Doctors and midwives are all aware of these faults and the machines are therefore constantly checked prior to use. Nevertheless, whenever a possible problem is identified, a check is carried out to make sure that the problem is not caused by a technical failure.

Another major disadvantage of continuous monitoring is that it restricts movement and confines women to bed. Some women find this makes their contractions more uncomfortable than if they are moving about and there is some evidence that posture can affect the length of labour, but it is only marginal. The use of telemetry (remote control), however, will overcome this problem when it is more reliable and more widely available. Unfortunately, there are difficulties with the present system and not many hospitals have it.

Who should be Monitored?

While some units may advise fetal monitoring of all women in labour because they feel it is safe, most agree that it is not necessary in every case, particularly in normal pregnancies. Some units think it advisable to monitor the baby's heart rate externally for a short time in early labour, and if this is satisfactory, to discontinue monitoring. It is common practice, however, to carry out continuous monitoring in induced labours and in pregnancies that have been complicated by blood pressure, diabetes, bleeding, also in premature labours, and where the baby's growth is thought to be affected. Under these circumstances it is advised for the safety of both the baby and mother.

Is there discomfort and pain for the mother and Baby?

There is no pain involved in monitoring for the mother at all, although some women undoubtedly find it uncomfortable to have to stay in bed during labour. There is no reason, however, why they cannot sit up and move about on the surface of the bed, although if the monitor is external it may lose the signal from the fetal heart and need repositioning. It is impossible to state categorically that there is no pain for the baby. If a fetal scalp electrode is used this device is designed so as not to damage the baby's scalp, and is usually applied with great care. There is certainly no reaction from the baby when it is attached.

11

Epidural Block

Barbara Morgan

The best methods of removing pain during labour is an injection of local anaesthetic into the epidural space, between the spinal cord and the backbone. This blocks the nerves and childbirth can then be free of pain, without dulling the alertness of the mother or the baby.

Whilst we are primarily concerned with childbirth it must be remembered that this anaesthetic block is also used for many patients having other forms of surgery. Epidural block has been used for pain relief since 1902, although it was not used much in the United Kingdom until the early 1970s. Since then it has been shown to be both safe and effective and it is used in most of the larger hospitals delivering babies.

It is particularly well suited to the pain of childbirth because by passing a very small plastic tube, or catheter, down a needle into the epidural space it is possible to give repeated doses of local anaesthetic without repeated injections. By 'topping-up' in this way the nerve block can last for many hours.

An epidural is also especially applicable to labour because the nerve block can be varied to a greater or lesser degree by changing the dose of local anaesthetic. It is thus possible to achieve a very slight block that takes away pain but still leaves an awareness of contractions and of the baby being born. This ideal is, nevertheless, difficult and indeed, at times, almost impossible to maintain. Yet by increasing the dose to cause a much more profound block a delivery by Caesarean section can be painlessly carried out.

It is the very versatility of this form of local anaesthetic that makes its use in childbirth such an important modern advance. It can be used to give the most strikingly successful pain relief in

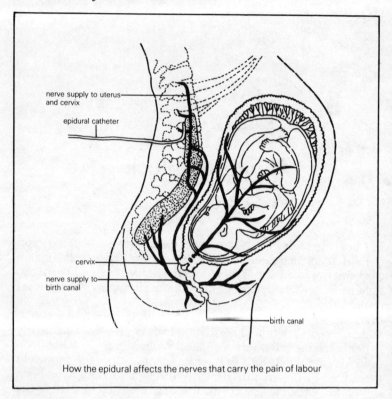

How the epidural affects the nerves that carry the pain of labour

normal labour, as well as an anaesthetic in complicated labour, and offers a safer alternative to general anaesthesia in labour.

How it is applied

The epidural space is surrounded by the spinal column and is approached from the mother's back. The process by which the space is entered is generally neither particularly painful nor time-consuming. It does, however, require a skilled anaesthetist who can insert it between contractions once labour is established. The mother will usually be asked to lie on her side with her knees bent as close to her tummy as possible and her chin on her chest, so that she is curled into a ball. Sometimes she may have to sit with her legs over one side of the bed. Once in the required position, the anaesthetist will prepare her back with a spirit solution, and having felt the bony landmarks in the small of the

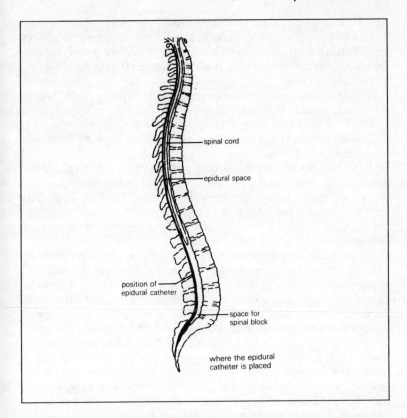

where the epidural
catheter is placed

back, will inject a small dose of local anaesthetic under the skin so that the epidural needle can be inserted with minimal pain.

Problems can occasionally arise when inserting the epidural catheter either if the mother is fat, making it difficult to feel the bony landmarks, or if the mother is unable to lie still and constantly pulls her back away from the anaesthetist because she is nervous or responding to a contraction. This is especially so when labour is advanced and it is difficult for her to keep still. Occasionally mothers have the sort of back that makes epidural catheterization difficult and this might be more painful than usual.

As soon as it is in place, a fine plastic tube is threaded through the needle, which can sometimes cause a sharp sensation like a slight electric shock down the leg which lasts for a few seconds. This results from the tube touching one of the nerves in the epidural space. The needle is then removed, leaving only the small catheter or tube running through the skin, which is then carefully strapped to the back. A small filter is placed on its free end, through which doses of local anaesthetic are given, usually by a midwife, at one- or two-hourly intervals under the direction of the anaesthetist.

Before a block is started several precautions must be taken. These are usually necessary because there is a possibility that the mother's blood pressure may fall once the local anaesthetic is injected, which would result in the mother feeling faint and nauseated and the baby possibly becoming distressed. To avoid this, intravenous fluid must be given to the mother before the epidural. This is done by placing a small plastic needle into a vein in her arm and infusing one or two bags of saline fluid. The midwife, under the direction of the anaesthetist, then measures the mother's blood pressure repeatedly after each dose of local anaesthetic.

To assess the possible effects of any drop in blood pressure on the baby it is usually necessary to monitor the baby's heart beat continuously before and after the block has started. The block can benefit the baby, but also have side effects. They can be two-fold. First the local anaesthetic drug is absorbed from the mother's epidural space into her bloodstream and passes to the baby; but as these drugs are in very low doses they do not appear to have a great effect on the baby as it can breathe and cry immediately it is born. The second effect, however, can be more serious: if the mother's blood pressure is lowered it reduces the baby's blood supply from the placenta; hence the checking of her blood pressure every five minutes, as already described.

Mothers are discouraged from lying on their backs with an epidural block because if the baby is lying over the mother's blood vessels, the blood pressure can drop, which may slow down the baby's heart beat.

There is no place for a partial epidural package. It is not sensible to wish for a painless labour with an epidural, but be unwilling to accept the intravenous drip, the electronic monitoring of the baby, the reduced ability to move around and adopt a position of one's choice, or the possible need for a forceps delivery and an episiotomy.

Complications

While the epidural block has been shown to be both safe and effective and is widely used throughout the country, the important limitation is the availability of trained anaesthetists. The anaesthetist must not only introduce the catheter but also be available in the event of complications. It is important that midwives and obstetricians understand the management of labour in women with epidural blocks; but please do not expect yours to have guaranteed success. It is, after all, like every other medical technique, subject to failure. It is very unlikely that an epidural block will cause you any damage, distress or paralysis, but it is not a dream machine. It is a highly technical anaesthetic process and accompanied by a variety of problems which can vary enormously from one person to another. It is a mistake to believe that it will ensure a painless labour for everyone.

A recent survey has shown that eighty-eight per cent of mothers who had an epidural in labour were 'satisfied' with the pain relief it gave them, but only fifty per cent had a completely painless labour. This is because success of the anaesthesia depends upon whereabouts in the epidural space the catheter comes to lie. Being flexible, it is inclined to bend when it is inserted and it is thus impossible to predict, and of course impossible to see, exactly where it will come to rest.

The result is that sometimes it may not work at all, or may work on one side only, or it may be inconsistent, giving patches of numbness and leaving patches of pain. Sometimes it fails because 'top-ups' are given too late. They are withheld in the hope that if the mother is allowed to regain sensation she may be better able to push the baby out. The anaesthetist must be on hand if the pain relief is unsatisfactory.

Another complication calling for the attention of the anaesthetist is if by accident the local anaesthetic drug enters into the space adjacent to the epidural space. This causes a total spinal block and is very rare indeed; most anaesthetists have never seen such a complication. It is, nevertheless, well-documented and feared, but if given prompt attention, no lasting harm will come to mother or baby.

During the epidural injection, the membrane lining the space can be penetrated, this is known as a dural tap, and often results in a very serious headache within the first day or two after delivery. This is mostly treated by bed rest and if it does not respond to this, a so-called blood patch is used. This is an injection of a small amount of the mother's own blood into the epidural space and almost always gives a complete cure to the headache. The incidence of dural tap is less than three per cent.

Some mothers have a morbid fear of being paralysed by an epidural block. This, of course, is a very serious complication and it has been recorded, but usually in the elderly patient having surgery. In the woman having a baby any form of nerve injury is remarkably rare, in fact, so rare that epidural blocks are considered safe, although like all anaesthetics great care is needed to reduce any problems to a minimum.

Another very rare complication is when a small portion of the plastic catheter is left in the epidural space after delivery. This is completely harmless and nothing needs to be done to retrieve it as the plastic is completely inert in the body. There is no evidence that bladder problems or backache are more common following an epidural block than after a labour and delivery without one.

Who should be receiving Epidural Blocks in Labour?

This is a subject of controversy and discussion among both doctors and midwives and mothers. Using epidural blocks in a labour that is or is likely to become complicated is generally approved by all. Twins, breech presentations, high blood pressure, previously difficult labours, poor progress in a very painful labour, or a baby that is very big or very small are all considered indications for an epidural block. When forceps delivery or a Caesarean section is needed or a placenta cannot be delivered, the mother is advised to have an epidural as this allows the treatment to be carried out painlessly without subjecting her to the risk of a general anaesthetic, which is considered to be less safe than an epidural for the mother and possibly for the baby as well.

It is generally felt that because epidural blocks are safe and provide the best pain relief any mother should be offered this option, providing a skilled anaesthetist is available throughout the labour. If she is keen to have one, if the anaesthetist is not attending to a more serious problem, and if her labour is not so far advanced that the baby will be delivered before the block takes effect, then most hospitals would agree that the mother ought to be given one. Where they are freely on offer about a third of mothers choose to have an epidural.

The argument against its use in normal labour is because of its effect on the labour itself. It can prolong the second stage and necessitate the use of forceps in first-time mothers. It seems important to point out to mothers, however, that they might have required a forceps delivery in a normal labour in any event. No harm is likely to come to mother or baby because of a forceps delivery, although it may leave some mothers dissatisfied with their experience of childbirth.

In an effort to reduce the need for forceps deliveries, various devices have been used: low doses of local anaesthetic; the block started late in labour; the mother left to have a longer second stage than usual, giving time for the baby's head to come down; and the block allowed to diminish and sensation return. None of these manoeuvres however, appears to make much difference. There is some evidence that increasing the strength of uterine contractions with a slow infusion of the drug Syntocinon can reduce the incidence of forceps delivery.

Contraindications

Some conditions discourage the use of epidural blocks in labour. When the mother is on anticoagulant drugs or suffers a problem with blood clotting, epidurals cannot be used. Women who are likely to bleed heavily are often advised against their use, as are those who have an infection with a high temperature.

More of a query is raised over mothers with unpredictable diseases like multiple sclerosis or other neurological conditions. Local anaesthetic drugs do not cause damage to nerves, but if the disease were to flare up after the delivery she would be likely to blame the epidural, especially if she had had no real handicap beforehand. Some anaesthetists, therefore, won't give epidurals to these women.

People with bad backs, previous back injuries or slipped discs are often anxious about epidurals. No association has been shown, however, between epidural block and an increase in, or relapse of, backache. Backache commonly occurs after childbirth anyway, often for the first time, whether the mother has had an epidural or not. There is also no evidence that the block is less likely to be successful where the mother has an existing back problem. If you have any condition which you are anxious about, you should discuss it with the consultant anaesthetist. You can usually make an appointment with him or her at the antenatal clinic.

After Effects

How long the effects last after the baby is born depends to some extent upon how long it is used before the birth, but sensation usually returns two to three hours after delivery. The bladder may take longer to function normally, but this is not unusual whether or not you have had an epidural block. You will feel pain following the episiotomy once the block has worn off, and likewise the after-pains of the uterus contracting down following the birth. Most mothers are able to walk within about twelve hours.

Side Effects

All drugs and anaesthetic techniques have some undesirable side effects; epidural blocks produce relatively minor ones. Mothers can feel nauseated and can vomit, although this is so common in labour that this could be considered normal, even without any drugs. Shivering is also common in labour, but can be worse following an epidural. Some mothers find the difficulty they experience in moving their legs an unpleasant or frightening sensation. It happens because of a nerve block to the leg muscles, but by using very diluted concentrations of the local anaesthetic, we attempt to delay this difficulty. The muscle-blocking effect will accumulate throughout the labour, however, especially if several 'top-ups' are needed. When larger doses, such as for forceps delivery or Caesarean section are required, then the muscle block is almost inevitable; but it should not last more than two to three hours after the baby is born.

Caesarean Sections

There is little argument that the epidural block is superior to general anaesthesia for Caesarean section. It is not only safe and effective, but it also allows the mother and father to participate in the birth of their baby. Its use means less post-operative pain and a speedier return of the mother to normal, also less drug depression of the infant. Many mothers are naturally anxious about having a Caesarean while awake and completely un-drugged; but they are not expected to be especially brave or watch the operation, and the experience will be no different from any other assisted delivery under epidural such as forceps. In most hospitals the father is allowed to stay as this often has a calming effect on the mother and allows them both to share the experience of the birth.

An epidural that is working perfectly will allow the mother to feel sensation, usually tugging or pulling with the delivery of the baby, but no pain. If the mother does experience pain, she should tell the anaesthetist, who will be with her throughout the procedure, and who will be able to treat it with the appropriate drug. Sometimes mothers experience pain for a short period, especially when the baby is about to be delivered. This is usually fleeting and either calls for no treatment, or for a few puffs of gas and oxygen.

Occasionally the block will be inadequate for surgery and the mother will have to be put to sleep with a general anaesthetic, but it should seldom be needed. In fact, in most hospitals three-quarters of all Caesarean sections are done with an epidural block, whether they are planned Caesareans or unexpectedly occur in the course of labour, with the result that the mother is able to breastfeed her baby as soon as the operation is over.

Availability

The epidural block itself is widely available in the United Kingdom, but its use is dependent upon the availability of anaesthetists. In the very small delivery units they are not usually available, but ninety-five per cent of all units which deliver more than five hundred babies a year, do offer an epidural service. Half of these units, however, are so short of anaesthetists that they can only provide a limited service, either on certain days of the week or at certain times, or for certain conditions. This is the only way these units can assure the safety of the mother.

Before booking into a delivery unit, therefore, it would be wise to ask the hospital about the extent of their epidural service. You can then assess your chances of being given an epidural if you need or want one during labour or for a Caesarean section. You might also like to make an appointment to see the consultant anaesthetist to discuss the unit's policy about epidurals, or talk to the parentcraft sister or midwife in charge about the midwives' attitude towards them.

In most units where they are freely available, the common sense attitude prevails: that is, in a labour which begins spontaneously, proceeds normally and in which the mother is able to cope with contractions using gas and oxygen if necessary, unless the mother insists on one, the use of an epidural is an unnecessary interference.

This is especially true in second or subsequent labours, which are usually quicker and so more tolerable than the first. Often in normal spontaneous labour the early part is often not sufficiently painful to bring the mother to hospital, and by the time she arrives her cervix is considerably dilated and she is able to continue her labour without an epidural and deliver with minimal or no analgesia.

12

Sexually Transmitted Diseases

Michael W. Adler

There are a number of sexually transmitted diseases that can affect the fetus and/or the newly born child. Most of these diseases, however, are not serious and in most instances transmission of the infection can be prevented. There are also some others which do not affect the child at all.

Infect the fetus	Infect the newborn	No infection of newborn
Syphilis	AIDS	Candida (thrush)
AIDS	Gonorrhoea	Trichomoniasis
	Chlamydia	Gardnerella
	Herpes	(anaerobic vaginosis)
	warts	

Syphilis

Syphilis is a very rare condition caused by a bacteria which can cross the placenta, so that the infection can occur in the womb before the child is born. In the adult the condition is spread through sexual intercourse. It can manifest itself in a number of ways:

1. Primary syphilis. This stage occurs within three months of sexual exposure to an infected person. The most common feature is a large single painless ulcer in the genital area. This will disappear without treatment, but the bacteria are still in the body so you can develop the next stage of syphilis, namely:

2. Secondary syphilis. This stage occurs approximately one to two months after the initial genital ulcer with a widespread skin

rash on the shoulders, chest, back, abdomen, arms, hands and soles of the feet. This rash is non-itchy and reddish-brown in colour. As with the lesion of primary syphilis it will disappear without treatment. Again, however, the bacteria are still in the body and can cause damage which may only show itself many years later (ten to twenty years) as the final stages of syphilis known as:

3. Tertiary syphilis – at this stage the heart and brain have become involved.

Since syphilis is an infection that can occur without you knowing that you have been infected, all pregnant women have a routine blood test at the antenatal clinic at the beginning of pregnancy to check this. It is highly unlikely that you have syphilis, and if you do, it is likely to be an infection with the early type, which is not serious. It is not serious because it can be treated with a course of penicillin; you will never have trouble again, and you will not suffer any of the later stages of syphilis. If, however, you are found to be suffering from the disease during your pregnancy it is virtually certain that the fetus will also have been infected; but don't worry because the treatment given to you will also treat the fetus, who will suffer no ill effects from either the treatment or the disease. You might have heard of congenital syphilis. This condition only occurs when a mother is not treated, but if she is, and adequately so, the baby will be cured and perfectly healthy.

In summary, therefore, syphilis is not a serious disease for you or your fetus as long as it is treated during the pregnancy with an adequate course of penicillin. The blood test alone in the antenatal clinic will indicate whether this is needed.

AIDS

This is a new disease caused by a virus called the human immuno-deficiency virus (HIV), which is spread by sexual intercourse with an infected person, and by blood and blood products contaminated with the virus. All blood is now screened in this country and is perfectly safe; so is the special preparation derived from blood that is given to haemophiliacs. Because of the ways in which the virus is currently spread in the United Kingdom, the groups particularly affected are homosexual men with multiple partners and intravenous drug addicts. However, all needles used to take blood from you and for giving injections are sterile and disposed of after they have been used, so there is no risk to you from having or giving blood and receiving injections.

Since the virus can be spread by sexual intercourse, heterosexuals could also be at risk. It has not yet spread into the heterosexual population at large in the UK, but if your sexual partner is a drug addict, a bisexual man, or has lived in an African country south of the Sahara in the last ten years, you could be at risk. Since it is not common amongst heterosexuals you will not normally be screened for AIDS during your pregnancy, but if you think you are at risk then it is important to discuss this with your doctor as soon as possible so that a test can be carried out if necessary. Some women become pregnant by artificial insemination, but most recognized centres will be screening all potential donors for evidence of infection with the virus. You should, nevertheless, ask whether this has been done.

If your blood test proves to be positive there is about a one in two chance that your fetus would also be infected. In view of this, you might consider having an abortion. If you decided against aborting, it is important to realize that your own health might be put at risk by continuing the pregnancy. Pregnancy in the healthy person alters the immune system (the system responsible for fighting infection) so that infection with this virus (which damages the immune system) at this stage will cause more trouble than at any other time. Thus, it's thought that pregnancy may increase the risk of progression to AIDS if you are infected with HIV. However, this has not been substantiated by studies. You might, however, wish to continue on the assumption that the baby has not been infected. The problem about this is that infection can still take place later on, possibly during labour, or while you are breastfeeding. Even though you should avoid breastfeeding, there is not much that can be done to avoid the possibility of infection during labour.

Being infected with the virus does *not* mean that you will definitely develop AIDS. At present it is estimated that about a third of people infected with HIV will develop the disease. Therefore, it is possible that you will have no problems, or that you may develop some other less serious manifestations of the disease, such as enlarged lymph nodes.

Gonorrhoea

Gonorrhoea is an infection, unlike syphilis and AIDS, that can only be transmitted as the baby actually passes down the birth canal, so the fetus is not at risk. It is spread through sexual intercourse, and the most common symptoms are vaginal discharge and occasionally abdominal pain and pain on intercourse, although the infection can be present without any symptoms. Gonorrhoea is not looked for routinely during pregnancy, but if it is discovered, you will be treated with a single course of penicillin and there should be no further problems or complications. It will be necessary, however, to examine your sexual contact(s) to exclude the same infection and offer treatment if necessary. This will avoid your being infected again or others becoming infected.

Since it is possible to have gonorrhoea with no symptoms, the first indication that you have it may be when the baby develops the infection. In such a case he or she would develop a red and swollen eye, or eyes, within a few days of birth. This looks awful, but can be treated early by penicillin and your baby will suffer no further problems.

Chlamydia

This bacteria is similar to gonorrhoea in that the fetus is never infected, only the newborn. The bacteria, *Chlamydia trachomatis*, is spread by sexual intercourse with an infected partner and exhibits the same symptoms as gonorrhoea, but, like gonorrhoea, can also produce no symptoms. Once again there is no routine screening during pregnancy, but if you are found to be infected you will be given a course of antibiotic tablets (erythromycin). Similarly, the first indication of infection may be through your baby. He or she could have a red swollen eye, or eyes, that may not appear until one to three weeks after the birth, and which look very like eyes that have been infected with gonorrhoea. Since the two look the same, but are treated differently, it will be necessary to take a swab from the eye to determine which it is.

Sticky eyes are common in newborn babies and they are not usually due to gonorrhoea or chlamydia, so should your baby develop a bad eye don't assume that you have infected it with a sexually transmitted disease.

As well as affecting the eyes, chlamydia can also involve your baby's throat, lungs and ears. He or she may not show signs of this for as long as three months after birth, although he will have been infected during delivery. He won't necessarily have a temperature, but he will develop a cough, which comes in bouts, rapid breathing and occasionally there will be a discharge from the nose and ears. This condition could be serious and must be treated with erythromycin which can be given orally in a liquid form to your baby.

Herpes

This is a virus which can affect the genital area, mouth and lips. Genital herpes is usually acquired by sexual intercourse; the most common way being through vaginal intercourse, but it can also be transmitted by orogenital contact with a partner who has lesions on the lips.

A first attack (primary herpes) usually produces many painful ulcers in the genital area. In most cases lesions occur both on the vulva and cervix, which are painful and tend to last about ten to fourteen days. Some people find that they feel unwell with a temperature, generalized aching and headaches. Once a person has been infected with the virus it remains in the body, and unfortunately most people will suffer from repeated attacks throughout their life. The only consolation is that these recurrent attacks are shorter and milder than the initial or primary attack. The rate at which they recur is very variable, some people having one attack every few years, others repeatedly every month.

There is no cure for herpes. A new antiviral drug called Acyclovir can stop the virus multiplying but will not rid the body of it, and since this drug is new and very expensive and its long-term effects are unknown doctors are not using it widely.

The fact that you suffer from genital herpes should not deter you from having a baby. In theory, it is possible for the virus to cross the placenta and infect the fetus, but the scientific evidence that this occurs in practice is very poor. If it does, it is likely that the infection would result in fetal death and spontaneous abortion. The main, and probably only, risk to the baby is during labour if an attack of herpes is taking place at the time. You are only infectious to your sexual partner and baby when the ulcers are present, because it is only at this time that you are shedding the virus. So if you were having an attack at the time of delivery the baby would come into contact with the virus while passing through the birth canal. To avoid this you would be offered a Caesarean section.

Herpes can be unpleasant, but however bad your attacks are, there should be no risk to your baby. It is important, however, that you tell the staff at the time of your first antenatal visit that you suffer from the disease. This will allow them to plan and discuss your management. Whatever happens, you should be monitored during the last four weeks of the pregnancy. This will mean weekly cultures being taken from both the cervix and vulva, even if there is no evidence of disease at the time.

Warts

Genital warts are caused by a virus, but it is a different type of virus from the one which causes warts in other parts of the body, such as the hands. They are nearly always transmitted by sexual contact, and it would be most unusual to infect oneself, for example, from warts on one's hands touching the genital area.

If you suffer from genital warts you might find that they increase in size during your pregnancy, which happens because of changes in your immune system. The usual treatment in the non-pregnant woman is a caustic agent called podophyllin, but this should not be used during pregnancy since it might be harmful to the fetus. You can use alternative therapy, such as freezing, or other caustic agents, or the warts can be left alone, because once the pregnancy is over they usually diminish in size of their own accord.

Very rarely they are so large that they obstruct the birth canal, in which case a Caesarean section will be necessary. The baby could become infected with the wart virus during a vaginal delivery, and develop warts in the throat, but this is extremely rare.

Other Miscellaneous Infections

There are a number of vaginal infections that can occur during pregnancy which do not infect the fetus or the newborn baby.

Candida
This is a common infection of the vagina caused by a yeast-like organism. The symptoms are an increased vaginal discharge, vulval irritation and soreness on intercourse. The condition is not usually sexually transmitted, but your partner may complain of a burning sensation and redness on the tip of the penis. Treatment is simple with a cream and pessaries (soft pellets that are placed into the vagina); and candida will not harm your baby.

Trichomoniasis/Gardnerella (anaerobic vaginosis)
These are two conditions that can be sexually transmitted, but are not always so. The symptoms are identical, namely an increased vaginal discharge and vulval irritation. Treatment in the non-pregnant woman is usually with a drug called metronidazole, but doctors do not like using this in early pregnancy because of potential harm to the fetus, or after delivery if you are breast-feeding because it gets into the milk. The alternative is not to treat the condition (it does not cause complications or long-term damage), although the symptoms may be so severe that something must be done. In that case, alternative therapies can be used, such as pessaries, but they are not as effective as metronidazole.

13
Unexplained Infertility

Ian D. Cooke

The term 'unexplained infertility' means different things to different people. Basically it means that after investigation no problem has been found that could explain why a couple remains infertile, but the extent and the quality of the investigation that is carried out varies considerably, therefore what further avenues are left to the couple also vary.

The Investigation

We consider that it is essential for both the male and female partner to have had a thorough history and physical examination before concluding that their infertility is unexplained. In the research centre at Sheffield we have a policy of accepting only married couples for further treatment. The basic investigations for the female are: an assessment of ovulation and an evaluation of tubal function.

Assessment of Ovulation
This involves the woman keeping a daily record of her temperature (basal temperature record) or taking a blood test for progesterone between days eighteen and twenty-five for regular cycles (from twenty-five to thirty-five days), with another for prolactin if the cycle is longer (to exclude the possibility of a pituitary tumour secreting the hormone prolactin, although it may also be raised by stress). A strip from the lining of the womb (endometrial biopsy) may also be taken, which would be done either as an outpatient or under general anaesthesia during a D & C (dilatation and curettage), so that the endometrium (lining of

the uterus) can be dated and assessed as consistent with ovulation.

Evaluation of Tubal Function
There are two ways of obtaining information about tubal function: by an X-ray of the womb (hysterosalpingogram), which also shows the shape of the cavity of the womb but gives little other information about the pelvic organs; or laparoscopy (inserting a telescope through an incision under the navel), which requires general anaesthesia. This won't tell us anything about the cavity of the womb, but it does provide comprehensive information about all the pelvic organs, the presence of adhesions, abnormalities of the tubal ends (which might make it difficult for the egg to get into the tube after release by the ovary) and the presence of endometriosis. This last is a condition in which fragments of the lining of the womb spill back through the tubes at menstruation and begin to grow on the back of the womb or on the ovaries.

Ideally both examinations should be done, and many would say that investigation is not complete unless a laparoscopy has been performed.

Evaluation of Semen
The male partner should have a semen analysis. Unfortunately, the standards of analysis vary enormously as does the interpretation. In addition, unless there are similar periods of abstinence (e.g. two to three days) before collecting each sample (by masturbation), the sperm density can also vary. Sperm movement (motility) and variations from ideal shape (morphology) are also significant. It is important to have more than twenty million sperm per ml of ejaculate, hence more than thirty per cent active motility with rapid forward progression, and more than forty per cent ideal shapes. These two indices require extremely careful analysis, and poor assessment of them accounts for many of the misinterpretations that occur.

Post-coital test
Finally a post-coital test is arranged. Ideally this should be just before ovulation when the cervical mucus is at its best. The mucus in the cervix is examined for the number of actively swimming sperm 'per microscope field of view' at high power (four hundred times magnification) between twelve and twenty-four hours after intercourse. However, ovulation is difficult to predict, so the timing may be wrong, the sperm numbers may be

inadequate or they may not be moving. The latter may be caused by poor quality sperm which could have been noted at an earlier stage if the semen analysis had been better. Nevertheless, there may be a few genuine problems of sperm/cervical mucus inter-action, for which treatment is uncertain.

If all these findings are normal there is a basis for making a diagnosis of unexplained infertility; but some couples who are referred with unexplained infertility simply need to complete the above investigations, and another diagnosis may emerge.

Prospects for Pregnancy

Once unexplained infertility has been diagnosed, the chances of becoming pregnant depend on whether you have previously been pregnant, on how long you have been infertile and to some extent your age, if you are over thirty-five years. If the infertility has already lasted two years and there has been no previous pregnancy, the prospect of pregnancy occurring will rise slowly to forty-two per cent over the next eight years. If there has been a previous pregnancy, all women with the diagnosis are likely to become pregnant over the next seven or eight years. There may be a small reduction in these figures with increasing age of the female partner.

It is difficult to know whether treatment makes any difference. If there is no obvious abnormality how can any treatment be rationally designed to deal with the problem? Yet drugs are widely used at this stage, e.g. clomiphene (Clomid), cyclofenil (Rehibin) or bromocriptine (Parlodel) or even gonodotrophins (Pergonal), and occasional pregnancies occur. From the figures just quoted, however, one would expect a few pregnancies to occur anyway, without treatment, and it is therefore difficult to attribute the pregnancies to the effect of the drugs. Certainly the few properly constructed studies using a control (placebo) do not show an increased pregnancy rate using these fertility agents. It is also probable that some of these treatments upset ovulation so much that pregnancy is actually prevented. We, therefore, do not use them in the treatment of unexplained infertility. Some of these drugs are used, however, in the treatment of ovulation disorders.

It is equally futile to use artificial insemination either of husband or of donor at this stage. The semen analysis should have demonstrated the normal quality of the sperm and the post-coital test will have shown that sperm can be deposited in the correct place: that is, intercourse is adequate, and the sperm are surviving and still swimming well.

If there is evidence that ovulation is occurring, there is no good reason to believe that psychological factors contribute to the problem. Tranquillizers and similar drugs may indeed act on parts of the brain that play a part in the hormonal control of ovulation, but research is still required to show that this leads to infertility.

We take the view that it is better to discuss the problem of the couple's infertility, explain the future prospects and give them a choice of four possible courses of action.

Possible Options

Adoption
The adoption process is currently fraught with difficulty because of the scarcity of babies for adoption, plus the arbitrary age limits of thirty-five, which are often put on each partner. If couples have started their attempt to conceive late in life, or have prolonged investigation into their infertility, then they may well be over the age limit when they come to think of adoption.

Adoption has been said to promote pregnancy, and, of course, this may be more likely in couples with unexplained infertility than in those with blocked tubes or absent sperm; but these stories are a hang-over from long ago when it was not necessary to have completed investigation before applying for adoption. There is no good evidence that adoption has this effect; and before considering it as an option, a couple must have accepted their infertility and have abandoned further investigation or 'treatment'.

In vitro fertilization (IVF)
In most areas of the UK this is an expensive option; waiting lists are long and successes are few. Nevertheless, as a process it can 'get round' some of the potential problems. If the problem really lies with the ovary, but the ovarian follicle containing the egg has developed, it may be possible to overcome the difficulty by removing the egg(s) artificially (as described in chapter 16). This gets round the process of follicle (egg) selection and that of egg release. It short-circuits the picking up of the egg by the tubal opening and exposes the egg to much higher concentrations of sperm. It also does away with the need for the fertilized egg to

pass along the tube, as the embryo is ultimately placed directly into the cavity of the womb. There may well be a serious problem with any of these processes, but so subtle that it was impossible to detect by the routine tests. So unexplained infertility may well represent a spectrum of minor abnormalities that effectively cause infertility, but which are not readily apparent; and by getting round those abnormalities by the use of in vitro fertilization, it may be possible to achieve a pregnancy.

Acceptance
A third alternative may be the couple coming to terms with their infertility, which means working through the grieving process implicit in this and modifying their lifestyles to build a life that is not centred around their own child or children. Reaching this decision may require considerable discussion and information counselling for attitudes to evolve. They can only emerge when realities and future prospects are clearly presented.

Join a research programme
The last option is to join a research programme where these problems are being further investigated. The principal objective of our own is to understand and explain the 'unexplained', but in the process of obtaining this information we may effectively include treatment (in vitro fertilization).

First there is a review of all information to date to fulfil the basic requirements outlined above and offer the options. Then there is a detailed explanation of what the further tests involve and how they are likely to provide diagnostic information to explain the problem, and finally, the programme provides a basis for selecting problems that seem amenable to defined treatments.

Next we need to carry out a more sophisticated semen analysis. In addition to the number of sperm, noted in the previous test, the number of a special type of cell (round cell) is counted and these are stained to distinguish immature sperm from white blood cells indicating infection. Their motility is graded and head, mid-piece and tail abnormalities are carefully described. The ability of antibodies to attach to motile sperm themselves is noted in the mixed antiglobulin reaction (MAR test) as anti-sperm antibodies are one cause of male infertility (see chapter 14). Sperm energy levels (ATP concentration) are assessed. The pH (acidity) of the specimen is carefully measured and the ability of washed sperm to swim in fresh solutions (sperm migration) is checked, which may suggest that the seminal fluid itself was exerting a detrimental effect.

The female's ovulatory cycle is then assessed further. A series of daily ovarian ultrasound scans is performed to identify the follicle and its pattern of growth. Blood samples are checked daily to measure oestradiol concentrations, which is the hormone produced by the growing follicle, to identify the luteinizing hormone (LH) surge, which triggers the pituitary gland to induce ovulation, and which is fired in turn by the pituitary assessment of the follicle's oestradiol production pattern.

Saliva, which is a new medium for assay of hormones, is collected daily to assess progesterone, and can be collected at home and stored frozen until the end of the cycle. It provides a pattern of the hormone back-up required to develop the womb lining (endometrium) to support implantation, the initial embedding of the embryo in the womb. It also provides better information to interpret than came from a single sample which might not have been ideally timed. In this way we can check the timing of the follicle in relation to the LH trigger and the start of the progesterone rise when it is at its maximum level before it ruptures or disappears. The LH surge can also be identified in urine by new technology dipsticks which change colour rapidly, allowing the timing of particular tests to be planned. Thus the cervical mucus testing can be securely timed, as can the post-coital test, and the timing of endometrial biopsy may be calculated to correspond to the time of predicted implantation to see if the endometrium is ideally developed.

These tests go a long way towards identifying the potential subtle problems, but even they may not cover every theoretical possibility. We know, for instance, that they do not explain about five per cent of the problems that we see. We believe, however, that interpreting these data for the couple plays an important part in the management of unexplained infertility, i.e. by their coming to understand that there is in fact some explanation for their continuing infertility.

We then consider whether the problem could be resolved by using in vitro fertilization (IVF). However, our approach to this technique is different from that found elsewhere, because we attempt at the same time to provide further details of any abnormality. Using the details of the ovarian cycle already gathered for the woman, and guided by ultrasound, we are now attempting to place a needle directly into the single unstimulated follicle, having given pain relief first. What we are trying to do is obtain not just an egg, but also the follicular fluid which can be subsequently analysed for hormones and growth factors. We then attempt to fertilize the egg with sperm already prepared from the woman's husband. If we are successful, and the rate of cell division is normal over the next thirty-six to forty-eight hours, we will then put the fertilized egg back into the womb.

If it fails, we check the information obtained at each stage to try and find a coherent reason. Excluding technical limitations, it is usually possible to indicate whether there is a major biological problem in either or both partners, and whether this problem could account for their long-standing infertility. If one is identified, we then consider whether it is biologically sensible to make a further attempt at IVF – whether IVF could ever get round the particular problem and allow a pregnancy to take place. In any case couples, who have always known that there must be some explanation for their infertility, usually get considerable satisfaction from discovering that there is some explanation, and seeing the abnormality demonstrated for the first time.

It seems that events within the ovarian cycle and indeed minor abnormalities in the semen tend to be reproduced within a particular individual, so that extrapolation from these monitored events appears to be valid. Acceptance of their infertility even without success with IVF or because of predicted failure at IVF therefore becomes somewhat easier, and for the first time capable of being understood. Problems that may be identified are: poor follicle growth, or inappropriate timing of the LH surge, which may come too early or too late; the oestradiol production from the follicle may be too low, or the follicle may not rupture on schedule; the hormone support of the corpus luteum (see p. 114) after ovulation (progesterone) may be poor but still greater than that found in those not ovulating (and described as a defective luteal phase); or the endometrium may not respond appropriately.

Treatments for these subtle defects that occur have not yet been established. Some that are used to stimulate ovulation when it is completely absent may not be appropriate in this context, but more research is needed to be sure. Sperm function may be found to be abnormal for the first time and if particularly severe, artificial insemination by donor may be suggested. There is no satisfactory evidence that artificial insemination using the husband's sperm provides any better prospect of pregnancy. Abnormalities of the seminal fluid have not yet been satisfactorily interpreted. Cervical mucus abnormalities are not usually found at this stage as a normal post-coital test is one criterion required for the diagnosis of 'unexplained infertility'. However, it may not previously have been done. Problems of poor follicle growth may account for poor mucus, or there may be antibodies in the mucus.

This can be discovered with 'sperm/cervical mucus interaction tests', where varying combinations of the patient's sperm and mucus and donor sperm and mucus are tested against one another, and antibody levels are checked to localize the problem to the sperm or to the mucus so that we can identify the source of the problem. Treatment at present is uncertain.

So-called 'unexplained infertility' currently reflects the lack of a diagnosis after preliminary testing. Further investigation is elaborate, time-consuming, often expensive, and may not provide an answer. It does seem likely, however, that the infertility suffered by most of the twenty-five per cent of infertile couples – which at present seems 'unexplained' – can be explained. They have subtle but important abnormalities. How they can be treated remains the immediate challenge.

14
Male Infertility

Lynn R. Fraser

Until recently infertility was considered to be due primarily to female-related factors, but evidence now indicates that approximately thirty to forty per cent of infertility is due to a male factor. It is also important to remember that, with a few exceptions which include total failure of the reproductive organs, infertility is a problem of couples; thus both partners should be investigated for contributing difficulties. For some individuals a change in partner can result either in successful conception or a failure to conceive.

Despite the common occurrence of male-related infertility, a proper investigation is not always carried out. This is surprising since a semen analysis is perhaps the easiest of available clinical tests to perform. However, some men are reluctant to be examined and they may find it difficult to come to terms with a diagnosis of male-related infertility. They often feel that their masculinity is threatened, despite the fact that in most cases no obvious physical symptoms are ever experienced.

The most common seminal problems include abnormalities in: ejaculate volume, sperm numbers, sperm motility (movement) and sperm morphology (appearance). A 'normal' ejaculate will have a volume of about two to six ml, averaging about four to five ml, which is roughly one teaspoonful. The average density will be fifty million sperm (or more) per ml, giving total numbers of two hundred million-plus sperm per ejaculate. Since only one sperm is required to fertilize an egg, this represents massive over-provision! However, it must be remembered that only a small proportion of sperm ejaculated into the vagina will actually be able to swim up into the cervical mucus and even fewer will swim out the other side into the uterus. Most will drain away out of the vagina when the semen liquefies about fifteen to thirty minutes after ejaculation. Given that a 'normal' ejaculate need only have fifty per cent normal forms and only fifty to sixty per cent need be actively motile, those initial millions are quickly reduced to much smaller numbers. Then, too, the further up the female reproductive tract we look, the fewer the numbers that reach the oviduct (or fallopian tube) where fertilization occurs. Since the end of the oviduct is open and connects with the main body cavity, sperm that have navigated the length of the tract will eventually leave it and will no longer have much chance of fertilizing an egg. At any one time, a maximum of a few hundred sperm will be available to attempt to fertilize an egg, if present. Thus any reduction in numbers of sperm introduced into the female tract might reduce the chances that conception will occur.

Causes of Infertility

The most common abnormalities encountered in male-related infertility are the absence of sperm in the ejaculate, the presence of relatively few sperm and immunological factors. These will be dealt with in turn. A fourth category, functional defects, will also be considered briefly.

Absence of sperm – azoospermia
The total absence of sperm in an ejaculate is indicative either of a failure in spermatogenesis, i.e. the testes are producing no sperm, or a defect/blockage of the male reproductive tract, i.e. sperm are being produced but cannot exit because of a fault in the ducts. Although biopsies of the testes used to be taken in order to assess spermatogenesis, today it is more common and more desirable to measure the circulating levels of the pituitary hormone FSH (follicle stimulating hormone). While clearly named for its function in females, it plays a vital role in males by stimulating testicular cells to maintain sperm production; FSH levels are often abnormally high in the absence of spermatogenesis.

Causes of this dysfunction include genetic disorders (e.g. Klinefelter's syndrome, where a male has sex chromosomes of XXY rather than the normal XY) and cryptorchidism (failure of testes to descend into the scrotum). In the latter case, early treatment may lead to normal sperm production; delayed treatment, even though the individual is prepubertal and would not yet be producing sperm, will lead to impaired function. Treatment should still be carried out, however, because the possibility of testicular cancer is significantly higher in men with undescended testes. Unfortunately, there is no cure for these types of azoospermia. Artificial insemination of donor semen (AID) can be offered as a possible treatment.

One other cause can be low levels of FSH and LH (luteinizing hormone) and appropriate administration of these hormones can reverse the condition. However, since such men essentially will have failed to undergo puberty, this condition is rarely seen in infertility clinics.

In men with either obstruction of the exit ducts or, occasionally, congenital absence of a part of the duct system, normal spermatogenesis occurs and FSH levels are normal. In at least some instances, the problem can be corrected by surgery, resulting in subsequent fertility.

Reduced numbers of sperm – oligozoospermia
Oligozoospermia is usually defined as the presence of twenty million sperm or fewer per ml of ejaculate and it is the most common abnormality found in infertile men. However, it must be remembered that this is simply a description of the semen characteristics and is not, in itself, a diagnosis. In many instances, no obvious cause for the reduced sperm numbers can be identified. A man who is termed oligozoospermic is not necessarily infertile, but his chances of achieving conception are statistically reduced compared to a man with normal sperm numbers. This is because oligozoospermic men generally have not only fewer sperm but a greater proportion of abnormal sperm as well. Both motility and morphology defects are common – the sperm may have very large or very small heads, two heads or two tails. All these are abnormal, some genetically so, and it would be undesirable for them to fertilize eggs. Fortunately, most such sperm are unable to reach the site of fertilization in the oviduct. Given the considerable reduction in sperm numbers at successively higher points in the female tract, oligozoospermic ejaculates are clearly at a disadvantage but it only requires one good sperm to be in the right place at the right time. Therefore, these men should be considered subfertile rather than infertile.

The causes of oligozoospermia can include: hormonal deficiencies, infection, varicose veins of the testes and drugs taken for therapeutic treatment (e.g. sulphasalazine to alleviate ulcerative colitis). The condition can be exacerbated by smoking, excessive alcohol, frequent very hot baths, tight underwear (e.g. Y-fronts) and 'social' drugs (e.g. marijuana).

Treatments often meet with variable success. If a hormonal deficiency can be identified (this is a fairly uncommon problem found in less than three per cent of infertile men), administration of the appropriate compounds may reverse the situation. Similarly, clearing up an infection can improve fertility and, in some men at least, surgical treatment of testicular varicose veins (varicoceles) can also lead to conception. If a therapeutic drug is the cause, it may be a decision as to whether the drug can be suspended for a short time or whether an alternative drug exists. In some men, the oligozoospermia may be the consequence of a severe attack of mumps after puberty; this can cause inflammation of the testes and irreversible damage to at least some of the sperm-producing cells. In such cases, nothing can be done to restore these cells.

Even when no clearly defined cause exists, it is possible to remove influences which may further reduce sperm production. These approaches include giving up smoking (there is a definite correlation between smoking and increased numbers of abnormal forms in the ejaculate) and reducing the intake of alcohol (excessive drinking may cause the production of incompletely formed sperm). It is well known from studies in laboratory animals such as rats that if scrotal temperatures were raised sperm production was decreased or even disrupted altogether. Normally, the scrotal temperature is slightly lower than that found inside the body. Therefore, very hot baths and tight underwear are better avoided. While such measures will not necessarily produce dramatic improvement, any positive steps may well help to increase the number of normal sperm.

If the cause of oligozoospermia cannot be identified, some general treatments have been reported to improve fertility, most notably the administration of the male sex hormone testosterone. Not many men are subfertile because they produce an inadequate quantity of testosterone and so small doses will have no positive effect. High doses of testosterone, however, completely suppress sperm production, and although this seems to be an undesirable response, quite the reverse of what you are trying to achieve, this method is frequently used to treat oligozoospermic men, because when the therapy is stopped, the man's own hormones take over control of sperm production and frequently produce higher numbers of sperm than ever they did prior to treatment. This is sometimes referred to as androgen (general term for male sex hormones) rebound therapy. The improvement is usually temporary, but may continue sufficiently long to allow conception. Repeat treatments are also possible.

Another approach is to collect split ejaculates and use these for AIH (artificial insemination of husband's semen). Ejaculation is not a single event but a series of pulsatile ejections of sperm plus fluid, with the initial fractions being richest in sperm. Using these for AIH will yield a higher sperm density and may improve fertility, but studies showing a significant increase in pregnancies have yet to be presented.

In vitro fertilization or IVF is another possibility. In many IVF clinics semen is routinely treated in a way to select only motile sperm before mixing with eggs. This is done either by placing a layer of culture medium over a volume of semen in a test tube and collecting the motile sperm that swim up into the medium, or by centrifuging the sperm in special fluids that collect the motile cells into one region of the centrifuge tube. Given that oligo-zoospermic semen often has a high proportion of poorly motile forms this approach enriches the proportion of normal cells. However, many clinics find that fertilization rates are frequently lower with such selected oligozoospermic samples than with normal samples. These results suggest that there may be some inherent defects in such sperm and at present we have no way of identifying and treating such deficiencies.

It has been suggested that semen samples exhibiting reduced motility might be treated so as to improve motility and then be used for AIH. Experimental studies have shown that washing sperm (from laboratory animals) and incubating them in compounds such as caffeine can result in increased numbers of motile cells. However, it is still at the experimental stage and has yet to be proved worthwhile. If all treatments fail, AID can be offered to the couple.

Immunological factors – antibodies to sperm
It has long been known that individuals can be immunized with sperm; that is, if injected with sperm both men and women can produce antibodies to sperm. While this might be expected in females, since sperm are clearly 'foreign' to them, it happens in males too, because sperm are also seen as 'foreign' by the man's immune system. This is because the immune system matures in the first few years after birth, but sperm are not produced until puberty at about the age of twelve; thus even in the male they are not recognized as 'self'. Normally contact between sperm and immunologically reactive cells is prevented but in some men the defences are breached and the presence of antibodies to sperm may be found in either serum or semen or both. Similarly, antibodies may also be detected in females. However, their

exposure to the antigens (sperm) is less frequent and therefore the responses in females are usually weaker.

Very high levels of antibodies in men may actually cause agglutination or clumping of sperm in the ejaculate. Since the sperm need to be freely motile to fertilize, this can have serious consequences for fertility. One major consequence when antibodies are present, either in semen or in female reproductive tract fluids, can be the prevention or impedence of sperm passage through cervical mucus. In severe cases, sperm cannot even enter the mucus, while in others, they enter but fail to make any progress: they simply twitch or shake. This can sometimes be detected by doing a post-coital test where, following intercourse, the cervical mucus is examined under a microscope for the presence of progressively motile sperm. The absence of sperm or the presence of non-progressing sperm may indicate antibodies. It has been suggested that in such instances the problem may be alleviated by direct insemination of sperm into the uterus, thus bypassing the cervical mucus. However, antibodies may also affect further progress up the female tract and/or actual penetration of the layers surrounding the egg.

Corticosteroids have been used with some success to improve fertility of men with antibodies to sperm. These drugs effectively depress the immune system and thus can cause a decrease, at least temporarily, in detectable antibody levels. In general, treatment is given during the first part of the female partner's ovulatory cycle so that the reduction in antibody production coincides with ovulation and thus, hopefully, increases the chances of conception. Since the drugs are quite powerful, they are not taken continuously for extended periods of time, but it is possible to have treatment during several ovulatory cycles.

Another approach that has been suggested involves washing of sperm to remove antibodies and then performing AIH. At present, however, there is no unequivocal evidence that this is a reliable way of improving fertility. It seems quite likely that many antibody molecules are actually bound tightly to the sperm and cannot be removed easily by washing.

If antibodies are detected in the woman, some studies have reported successful conceptions after the use of condoms for several months. The theory is that by preventing contact between sperm and the female tract, antibody levels will decline and chances of conception will rise. Further investigation is required to prove that this is a reliable method of treatment, but it is a very easy approach to try.

Functional defects
Some men produce normal numbers of sperm but remain infertile. Obvious problems can be identified if most sperm are abnormally shaped or if motility is either very poor or absent. However, more subtle defects may account for infertility in other men. We know from work on other species that mammalian sperm are not fertile immediately upon release from the male; even if such sperm are mixed directly with eggs they cannot fertilize. A series of poorly understood changes must occur in the sperm, over a period of several hours, before they become fully fertile. It is probable that some men are infertile because their sperm cannot complete these changes. At present, methods for detecting such individuals are being sought. The possibility of treatment, at least in some cases, may exist in the future but probably not for some time; currently, only AID could be offered.

Conclusions

Infertility due to a male factor contributes significantly to the overall incidence of infertility. However, although some men can be treated successfully, it must be said that the general picture is less positive than for women with fertility problems. In large part this reflects the basic differences in hormonal control in the two sexes. Females have a monthly cycle of hormone changes which regulate ovulation and often their infertility is due to alterations in hormones which disrupt ovulation. If the normal hormone patterns can be re-established, normal ovulation will occur and conception may ensue. Males have a continuous production of hormones, i.e. no cyclicity, and therefore the defects that occur are often more fundamental and not so easily reversed. Nevertheless, the clear acknowledgement of male factors in infertility and the move towards evaluation and treatment of couples, rather than just one partner, has led to considerable improvement in treatments currently available and new methods are constantly being sought.

15
Disorders of Ovulation

Stephen Franks

Disorders of ovulation are an important cause of infertility and also of disturbances of menstruation. Recent advances in areas such as hormone measurements and ultrasound examination of the ovaries and uterus have meant that we are able to make a precise diagnosis of the cause of failure of ovulation in almost all patients. Similarly, progress in finding new methods for stimulating ovulation has enabled us to choose effective treatment for women with these disorders.

In order to understand where things may go wrong in the process of ovulation, it is helpful to have some knowledge of how normal ovulation occurs.

The Normal Menstrual Cycle

The normal menstrual cycle lasts on average twenty-eight days, but there is a good deal of variation between women in the length of the cycle. For example, it is possible to have normal ovulatory cycles lasting as short as twenty-one days or as long as thirty-five days, but usually there is no more than a four-day variation from month to month. Irregular cycles do not necessarily mean that ovulation has failed to occur, but if your cycle is irregular you have a greater chance of having a disturbance of ovulation. Ovulation is the process by which a mature egg is released from the ovary. Usually only a single egg matures sufficiently each month to be released from its follicle. At the beginning of each period the ovary contains several follicles, which can be identified on ultrasound, but usually only one follicle will continue to grow; in the seven days before ovulation it doubles in size from a diameter of 10 mm to 20 mm (approximately the size of a 5p piece) at the time of ovulation. Ovulation usually takes place about two weeks after the start of a period. The follicle wall becomes very thin; there is a pin-point rupture in the surface of the ovary and the egg is released to be picked up by the fallopian tubes. After release of the egg the collapsed follicle develops a very rich blood supply and becomes what is known as the corpus luteum. If the egg is fertilized and attaches to the womb a hormone called human chorionic gonadotrophin (HCG) is released which keeps the corpus luteum active. The presence of this hormone in the circulation is the basis of the blood or urine tests used for diagnosis of early pregnancy. The hormone activity of the corpus luteum is important for maintaining early pregnancy. If, however, fertilization does not occur, the corpus luteum has a limited life-span (about fourteen days). When the hormone activity of the corpus luteum wanes the endometrium or lining of the womb, which is sustained by these hormones, becomes fragile and detaches itself, leading to menstruation. At this time new follicles are forming in the ovary and the cycle can start again.

This cycle of events in the ovary is controlled by two of a family of hormones called gonadotrophins; they are produced by the pituitary gland, and are called luteinizing hormone (LH) and follicle stimulating hormone (FSH). They control first the growth of the follicle, then ovulation and finally the activity of the corpus luteum, which is also controlled by HCG. The hormones made by the ovary itself are therefore carefully controlled by the pituitary gland. In the first half of the cycle leading up to ovulation the main hormone produced is oestradiol (an oestrogen) (see A on diagram). This hormone has a number of important functions. It helps to provide the right hormone environment for the egg to mature. It gives a hormone signal to the pituitary to trigger the surge of LH (see B on diagram), which leads to ovulation; it builds up the endometrium and it changes the mucus in the cervix (neck of the womb) to allow easy passage of sperm at the time of ovulation (see C on diagram). In the second half of the cycle the corpus luteum makes a hormone called progesterone (see D on diagram) and also continues to make oestradiol. A combination of progesterone and oestradiol conditions the endometrium to receive the fertilized egg. If pregnancy occurs and the corpus luteum carries on working it is progesterone which is important for maintaining the correct environment within the uterus.

We now know that the release of gonadotrophins from the pituitary gland is itself controlled by a hormone released from a

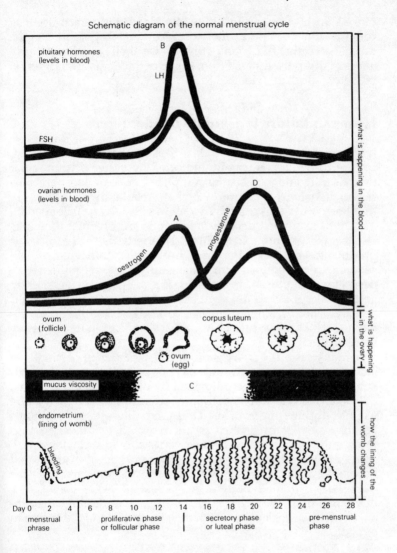

Schematic diagram of the normal menstrual cycle

specialized part of the brain called the hypothalamus. The hypothalamus lies directly above the pituitary gland at the base of the brain. The hormone called gonadotrophin releasing hormone (GnRH or LHRH) is manufactured in specialized nerve cells in the hypothalamus and is released in pulses into tiny blood vessels which transport the hormone directly to the pituitary. Recently we have come to realize that these pulses (which may be picked up by measuring LH in the blood and which occur at roughly ninety-minute intervals) are very important for the normal secretion of LH and FSH. As we shall see later, disturbances in this pulsed signal from the hypothalamus are a common cause of failure to ovulate.

How can failure to Ovulate be identified?

If a women has regular periods it is likely that she is ovulating. Failure to ovulate is usually indicated by either very irregular periods (oligomenorrhoea) or complete lack of periods (amenorrhoea). Obviously, failure to ovulate results in infertility, but there are other reasons why women who have problems with ovulation may need help. If the periods are irregular they may also be very heavy and painful. This is because the ovary is producing only oestrogen and not progesterone. As a consequence the endometrium builds up under the influence of oestrogen, but unless progesterone is also produced it carries on getting thicker and is not shed at the right time. At some point, usually when oestrogen levels fall slightly, the lining of the womb, which may then be very thick, is shed, causing heavy bleeding.

In many cases the ovary is producing insufficient oestrogen to stimulate the endometrium, so no periods occur. Indeed, amenorrhoea may be accompanied by other signs of oestrogen deficiency such as hot flushes and a dryness and soreness of the vagina during intercourse. These are important symptoms because even if pregnancy is not required it is necessary to replace the oestrogen which the ovaries should be making.

In some cases there may be symptoms or signs of an associated hormone disturbance in women who do not ovulate: for example, unwanted body hair, persistent acne, or a milky discharge from the breast (galactorrhoea), indicating disturbances of other hormones which may be relevant to the failure to ovulate.

Disorders of Ovulation – Causes

Failure to ovulate therefore can be due either to disorders of the ovaries themselves or to a disorder in the hormone signal from the pituitary to the ovary. If the problem arises from the ovary itself (primary ovarian failure) there is little that can be done to ensure normal ovulation. Fortunately this form of failure to ovulate occurs in only about ten per cent of women who suffer from amenorrhoea. The malfunction of the ovary is similar to that which occurs during the natural menopause and for this reason this form of ovarian failure is sometimes referred to as 'premature menopause'. Recently it has been shown that about one in five women with primary ovarian failure may experience a return of their periods, and although these patients rarely have regular ovulatory cycles the occasional pregnancy has been reported.

It is hoped that this group of women will benefit in due course from the new techniques of in vitro fertilization (see below and chapter 16) which will allow eggs to be frozen and thawed successfully. This will mean that eggs will be available (from a donor) for a woman who is unable to ovulate herself. The egg, fertilized by her partner's sperm, can then be placed in the womb after the patient has received suitable hormone preparation. A handful of successful pregnancies using freshly recovered eggs have already been reported, but it will be some time before this technique becomes generally available. The mainstay of treatment for women who have primary ovarian failure is oestrogen replacement. The most convenient way to give this is either in the form of the combined oral contraceptive or using one of the low dose hormone replacement combinations which are available for menopausal women. Oestrogen replacement is important, not only to relieve any hot flushes or vaginal soreness, but also to prevent premature thinning of the bones (osteoporosis). This is discussed further in chapter 23.

In the majority of women with failure of ovulation the problem lies in the ovary receiving a deficient or inappropriate signal from the pituitary. Perhaps the most common disorder in this group is the so-called 'polycystic ovary syndrome'. This term is used to describe failure of ovulation, presenting as amenorrhoea, or more commonly, oligomenorrhoea associated with a characteristic appearance of the ovary. Until recently the precise definition of the ovarian appearance of polycystic ovaries depended on examining the ovaries at laparoscopy (inserting a telescope into an incision under the navel) and perhaps even taking a biopsy (tissue sample) of the ovary. Both procedures involve a general anaesthetic. Fortunately, it is now possible to use pelvic ultrasound scanning to make the diagnosis. The polycystic ovary is probably a variation of normal: the 'cysts' are in fact follicles which, of course, are normal structures within the ovary. It is usually enlarged and this is because there is an increase in the number of follicles and in the amount of stroma or 'packing tissue', in the ovary.

Polycystic ovaries have been found in more than half of the patients with ovulatory failure that we have investigated and are clearly the most important cause of such disorders. There are often other clues to the diagnosis, however, such as unwanted hair growth and a characteristic hormone imbalance in the blood test. The ovaries secrete relatively more androgen (male hormone) than normal, but it is important to realize that androgens are made in large quantities even by normal ovaries. In fact, the ovary could not make oestrogen without first making androgens. It is the slight excess of androgen leaking into the circulation which tends to cause acne or unwanted facial hair. Because the definition of polycystic ovaries on ultrasound involves a high degree of skill and experience the diagnosis is quite often made on the combination of symptoms and character-istic abnormalities in the blood tests. Why polycystic ovary syndrome should cause a failure in ovulation is not entirely clear, but the most likely explanation is that the ovary is not receiving the right signal of follicle stimulating hormone (FSH) from the pituitary. The aim of treatment, therefore, is to increase the output of FSH from the patient's own pituitary gland, or to give extra FSH by injection (see below).

Low levels of LH and FSH or an abnormal pulse pattern of these hormones are characteristic of a large number of disorders of ovulation. In these circumstances the patient usually experiences a complete lack of periods and sometimes quite marked symptoms of oestrogen deficiency. One of the most important causes of this disturbance is weight loss. Women with anorexia nervosa and severe weight loss have very low levels of LH and FSH, but even with milder degrees of weight loss and during the recovery phase of anorexia nervosa, the signal from the hypothalamus to the pituitary is so disturbed that ovulation cannot occur. It is very important to recognize the association between being underweight and lack of periods, because in most cases ovulation can be restored by gaining weight. This is not quite as easy as it sounds because many such patients will require help with underlying psychological disturbances in order to cope with weight gain. Some patients still do not experience a return of periods even when they have returned to a normal weight. In such cases ovulation can be induced by giving gonadotrophin injections or, more naturally, by giving gonadotrophin releasing hormone (GnRH) in a pulsatile infusion pump (see below).

A disturbance in the regulation of LH and FSH is also seen in women who have raised levels of prolactin in the blood. Prolactin is another pituitary hormone whose main role is to stimulate milk production after pregnancy. But if prolactin levels are raised when they should not be (i.e. other than during pregnancy and lactation) the result is similar to the effect of raised prolactin levels during breastfeeding. In other words, menstruation is switched off and some women even develop inappropriate milk secretion (galactorrhoea). The raised levels of prolactin seem to disturb the normal pulse pattern of gonadotrophin secretion, but normal pulses and therefore normal ovulation can be restored by lowering prolactin levels to normal using a drug called bromocriptine (see below).

There are a variety of other factors which can disturb the signal from the hypothalamus to the pituitary and so deprive the ovary of the normal gonadotrophin stimulus. These include a very strenuous exercise programme (an increasingly important cause of amenorrhoea), stress, such as taking examinations or moving house and chronic illness (such as kidney failure). In each of these cases the main aim of treatment is to correct the underlying problem, but when this is not possible it may be desirable to use one of the other methods for stimulating ovulation as described below.

Treatment

The principles of treatment have already been discussed. It is very important to make the correct diagnosis and choose the most suitable treatment accordingly. If this principle is adhered to, then, with the exception of patients with primary ovarian failure, normal fertility can be achieved in most cases. In mild disturbances of the hormone signal to the ovary it may be sufficient to give a drug which stimulates the pituitary to produce its own LH and FSH. A good example of such a drug is clomiphene.

Clomiphene
This is an 'anti-oestrogen', similar in structure to natural oestrogen, which is only usually effective when the levels of oestrogen in the circulation are not too low, for example, in women with polycystic ovary syndrome and after recovery of weight loss. It is given in the form of tablets, usually starting within three days of a period. The pituitary produces LH and FSH in response to clomiphene and the rise in follicle stimulating hormone will, as the name suggests, lead to development of a large follicle from which ovulation can occur. In properly selected patients this treatment is simple and effective. Side effects do

occasionally occur, the most common of which are headaches and hot flushes, but these are usually short-lived and will not put the patient off treatment. If treatment with clomiphene fails to induce ovulation, this must be identified as soon as possible and treatment re-assessed. It may be that there is a more severe deficiency of pituitary gonadotrophins than was first realized in which case treatment with gonadotrophin injections or pulsatile GnRH may be required (see below). But there is also a group of women with polycystic ovary syndrome, who, despite normal or even raised levels of LH and normal concentrations of FSH, fail to ovulate in response to clomiphene. In these women, treatment with low doses of gonadotrophins by injections may be the most appropriate form of management (see below).

Bromocriptine
This is a drug which acts like the natural control mechanism for prolactin. It is therefore very effective when given to patients with raised prolactin levels. When the levels are reduced to normal, ovulation resumes. This drug is given twice or three times daily, but, in contrast to treatment with clomiphene, it must be given continuously. Side effects when starting treatment are quite common (principally nausea, dizziness on standing upright and stuffiness of the nose), but these side effects are much less troublesome if the drug is started at a low dose and gradually increased. If the tablets are taken with meals this also helps. In any case, the side effects usually wear off within a few days. Sometimes patients with an increased amount of prolactin from the pituitary suffer some enlargement of the pituitary gland and it is fascinating to note that bromocriptine is also able to shrink the pituitary to normal size as well as lowering prolactin levels. This means that it is rarely necessary to perform surgery on the pituitary gland to lower prolactin levels as was the case a few years ago.

Gonadotrophin injections
The most commonly used preparations of gonadotrophin are human menopausal gonadotrophin abbreviated to HMG (Pergonal) or urofollotrophin (Metrodin). Both are natural hormones extracted and purified from urine, but they are of course derived originally from the pituitary. The difference between Pergonal and Metrodin is that Pergonal contains equal amounts of LH and FSH, whereas Metrodin contains only FSH. Metrodin is usually reserved for treatment of women with polycystic ovary syndrome who often have high levels of LH and

therefore do not require the extra LH which is contained in Pergonal. We have found that Metrodin is particularly effective when given in a low dose, which is then gradually increased until the ovaries begin to respond. It is not clear yet whether Metrodin really does have any advantage over Pergonal for treatment of women with polycystic ovaries, but research into this question is in progress.

Pergonal treatment is especially successful in women who fail to ovulate because the pituitary is not making adequate amounts of LH and FSH. The main problem with gonadotrophin injections in this situation, and, particularly in women with polycystic ovaries, is that stimulation of multiple ovulation often occurs. Multiple pregnancy may seem, at first sight, an attractive proposition for the infertile patient but, unfortunately, the chances of a successful outcome are much less than if a single pregnancy is achieved. For this reason we always try to minimize the chance of overstimulating the ovaries by carefully watching the response to gonadotrophin treatment. This may mean regular ultrasound scans of the ovary, measurement of oestrogen levels in blood or urine or a combination of these two methods. When a mature ('ripe') follicle is achieved, the actual process of ovulation is triggered by giving an injection of HCG, which in this case acts like LH.

Pulsatile GnRH
It should be remembered that a failure in the gonadotrophin signal to the ovary is in most cases secondary to a disturbance in GnRH pulses from the hypothalamus. It therefore seems more logical to use GnRH itself to induce ovulation. One of the most exciting developments in the last few years has been the use of miniaturized battery-driven pulsatile infusion pumps to deliver pulses of GnRH in order to stimulate first the pituitary and then the ovaries. The pumps are the size of a pack of cards and contain equipment capable of delivering a dose of gonadotrophin releasing hormone from a reservoir directly into the woman's bloodstream at specifically timed intervals. Generally, they are strapped to the upper arm or waist. This is a more 'natural' method of inducing ovulation because it allows the normal signals between the pituitary and the ovary to be preserved. As a consequence, the chances of overstimulating the ovary and producing many follicles are much reduced. Many successful pregnancies have resulted from the use of the pulsatile infusion pump for this purpose.

As mentioned previously, not all women with disorders of

ovulation will require pregnancy and there are other reasons for treatment. If periods are irregular, heavy or painful it is important that menstruation is regulated. This can usually be effected by giving synthetic progestogens (hormones which are like natural progesterone). Effective control of the periods can often be achieved simply by giving a low dose combined oral contraceptive (see chapter 21). This form of treatment is also very suitable for women who have symptoms of oestrogen deficiency related to underactivity of the ovaries.

Where to go to for treatment
The principles of diagnosis and management of disorders of ovulation are simple, but to practise adequate investigation and treatment a clinic must be able to provide expert clinical advice, as well as laboratory back-up and facilities for induction and monitoring of ovulation. It is therefore important to choose a centre where such facilities are available. Most of these centres are concentrated in university teaching hospitals.

16

In Vitro Fertilization, GIFT, POST and DIPI

Brian A. Lieberman

In vitro fertilization (IVF), gamete intrafallopian transfer (GIFT), and other variations on the 'test-tube' baby technique, are complex procedures. What is described here is the basic system followed in Manchester, but variations exist between different IVF services. The purpose of this chapter is to answer many of your questions and give some insight into the procedures involved in treatment.

The media make these processes sound very simple, but in reality they are complicated and very time-consuming. Before treatment is started investigations are necessary to ensure that you are suitable, and invariably some months will pass before a treatment cycle is started.

Embarking on a treatment will keep you very busy from about the eighth or ninth day of the cycle, with daily trips to the hospital for blood tests, urine collections and ultrasound scans. You will require time off work, and it is also a good idea to plan ahead and stock your freezer with pre-cooked meals, for example. Treatment is designed to achieve a pregnancy, so if you smoke, stop now, and make sure you are eating a healthy well-balanced diet.

A lot of people are involved in the team. Some work behind the scenes; others you will meet on your visits to the hospital, and they will go to great lengths to keep you informed about your progress. If there is anything you do not understand, you should ask; since treatment is tailored to the individual, do not be surprised if other women are being treated differently.

It is very important to remember that the 'test-tube' technique and GIFT fail more often than they succeed, and if things don't go

	Reproductive Disorder	Ovarian Stimulation	Method of Egg Collection	Replacement of Eggs, Sperm or Embryos	Outcome	Complications
IVF	*Female:* Blocked, absent or damaged tubes. Endometriosis. *Male:* Some cases of reduced sperm counts on motility.	Necessary to improve chances of pregnancy, normally clomiphene followed by H.M.G. (Human Menopausal Gonadotrophin)	By laparoscopy (general anaesthetic) or ultrasound (local or general anaesthetic)	No anaesthesia neccessary. Embryos replaced into womb 2-4 days after recovery.	12-30% pregnancy rate per treatment cycle.	Multiple pregnancy 20% Miscarriages rate of up to 30% Ectopic pregnancy 2-3%
GIFT	*Female:* Unexplained infertility with normal tubes. Cervical mucus hostility. Pelvic endometriosis not affecting the tubes. *Male:* Some cases of reduced sperm counts or motility. Anti sperm antibodies.	As with IVF	Always by laparoscopy under general anaesthetic	Eggs & sperm replaced into fallopian tube at time of egg recovery.	30-35% pregnancy rate per treatment cycle	Rate of miscarriage similar to IVF. Ectopic rate in excess of 3%. Multiple pregnancy as with IVF
POST	As with GIFT	As with IVF	By ultrasound under local anaesthetic	Injected into pelvis under local anaesthetic immediately following recovery.	Similar to GIFT. Preliminary reports only.	Likely to be similar to GIFT
DIPI	Unexplained infertility. Some male disorders. Cervical mucus hostility.	Clomiphene only or natural cycles.	Spontaneous ovulation.	Sperm only injected into pelvis under local anaesthetic.	Pregnancy rate of 10-15% per cycle.	Lower than with IVF, GIFT or POST

according to plan, the treatment may have to be abandoned at any time. You should not, therefore, allow yourself to build up hopes falsely. Coping with this disappointment is difficult and many couples find it very hard to come to terms with yet another unsuccessful infertility treatment.

The reasons for failure vary. Sometimes they are obvious, like the inability to obtain oocytes (eggs) at laparoscopy or by scan. In other cases it's a mystery, and if everything seems to have gone according to plan, and menstruation then occurs, it's very disappointing and depressing. Not knowing what went wrong often makes it harder for the woman to accept.

What is IVF?

In vitro fertilization literally means that the egg and sperm are put together outside the body in a glass dish or test tube.

In a natural ovulatory cycle a single egg develops in an ovary; it grows in a fluid-filled cyst (a follicle) until it is 'ripe', when it is released (ovulation) and passes down the fallopian tube. The developing follicle produces hormones which can be measured in the blood, and the size of the follicle can be seen on ultrasound scans.

Normally the egg and sperm meet in the fallopian tube and fertilization results in the formation of a conceptus (or pre-embryo). As the conceptus travels down the tube to the womb (uterus), the cells divide and grow. If a pregnancy is established, the embryo will start to implant into the lining of the womb about seven days after the egg is released.

IVF was developed to help women whose fallopian tubes were damaged, by taking the egg from the follicle just before it is ready to be released, fertilizing it in the laboratory, and replacing the conceptus into the womb several days later. The procedure is also of use in some cases of male infertility, and where there is no obvious cause (unexplained infertility, see chapter 13).

How IVF is performed

There are several stages, and problems which result in the treatment being abandoned may occur at any one of them.

Stimulation of egg production
The chances of pregnancy are increased if more than one egg is

recovered and several concepti replaced. Thus the ovary is stimulated by anti-oestrogen tablets (e.g. Serophene or Clomid) and probably by injections of Pergonal to increase the number of eggs produced. Everyone responds differently, so the time, dose and type of stimulation varies between patients.

Monitoring egg development
Daily blood tests are taken to measure the levels of hormones produced by the follicle; and ultrasound scans help to show the number of follicles developing and to assess their maturity. The time of ovulation is controlled by an injection of human chorionic gonadotrophin (HCG), which is given thirty-four to thirty-six hours before oocyte (egg) recovery. Urine collections are started a few days before this to monitor the body's own ovulating hormone.

Egg recovery and fertilization
Eggs are removed from the follicles either by laparoscopy (under general anaesthesia) or by using the ultrasound scan to guide a needle into the follicles (under general or local anaesthetic). The eggs are then placed in a special solution which provides essential nutrients. A fresh semen sample is prepared to select the most motile sperms; these are then added to the egg(s) and incubated overnight. The eggs are examined the next day to see if fertilization has taken place, and if so, the concepti are incubated for a further twenty-four to forty-eight hours.

Embryo replacement
This is a painless procedure and does not require an anaesthetic. Only those concepti which are developing normally are put back into the womb. If more than one is replaced, the chances of success are higher, but so too are the risks of multiple pregnancy. We recommend replacing up to three, but in certain exceptional clinical circumstances (such as women who have never been pregnant before – primary infertility), or where this will be the last or only attempt at IVF we may replace four concepti. Once they have been replaced, you should rest for a few hours, and don't take part in any strenuous activity, or have intercourse, until the outcome of the treatment is known.

What are the chances of success?
About fifteen per cent of women who reach this stage of replacement become pregnant. Almost thirty-three per cent of these pregnancies may miscarry, and between one and three per

cent may end as an ectopic pregnancy (where the embryo implants outside the womb). Miscarriages occur quite commonly in normal pregnancies too, but we are more aware of them after IVF treatment because the pregnancy is diagnosed at a much earlier stage. If more than two concepti are replaced, the probability of implantation goes up to about twenty-five per cent. Great care needs to be exercised when trying to gauge the chances of success, however, because there are so many variable factors. a) The implantation rate and 'baby take-home rate' vary according to the rate of miscarriage, and the rate of chromosome abnormalities, both of which become more likely in older mothers. b) The actual cause of the infertility is significant. For example, women who have been pregnant before (secondary infertility) are more likely to become pregnant after IVF than those who have never been pregnant. c) The presence of a 'male factor', i.e. poor semen quality, also reduces the chances of success quite significantly. It is important to check with the clinic that the rates quoted reflect all couples who have been treated and have reached the stage of replacing the eggs, as different units use different criteria to assess their success.

There is no evidence to suggest that the risk of abnormalities in babies born after IVF is any higher than in a normal pregnancy.

What it involves

The following schedule is an example of a typical treatment cycle. Units are constantly trying to improve methods and there may well be differences when you are ready for treatment.

DAY
1 Start of period; ring to inform unit if available for treatment.
2 Start taking Serophene or Clomid tablets at 08.00 hrs. and 16.00 hrs. for five days.
5 Start Pergonal injections at 16.00 hrs., 2 ampoules.
6 Two ampoules Pergonal at 16.00 hrs.
7 Two ampoules Pergonal at 16.00 hrs.
8 Attend hospital for blood test at 08.30 hrs. followed by a scan. Possibly more Pergonal at 16.00 hrs. Early morning urine sample.
9 Blood test 08.30 hrs. Start 3-hourly urine collections.
10 Blood test 08.30 hrs. followed by a scan. Return for HCG (profasi or Pregnyl) injection between 21.30 and 23.30 hrs.
11 Blood test 08.30 hrs. Continue with 3-hourly urine collections.

12   Possible admission at 07.30 hrs. for egg recovery.
13   Discharged after fertilization check.
14   Ring IVF Unit between 14.00 and 15.00 hrs. to check that conceptus is dividing.
15   Readmitted 09.00 hrs. for replacement. Discharged after dinner.
22, 24, 26   Blood tests at GP or Unit to check if implantation has occurred.
28–30   Ring Unit to inform if a period starts.
33   Scan if menstruation has not started.
NB. This is only an example to give you a general idea of a typical programme.

   If treatment is not successful the first time, we usually advise another attempt four to six months later.

What is GIFT?

Gamete intra fallopian transfer (GIFT) is only suitable for women with apparently normal tubes. It is a procedure similar to IVF, but instead of the egg and sperm being placed together in a test tube, they are replaced into the woman's fallopian tubes (up to two eggs per tube) while she is anaesthetized immediately following the egg retrieval.

   GIFT is more successful than IVF, but the risk of ectopic pregnancy is greater. Pregnancy rates of about thirty per cent are reported. It is our present policy with some male disorders to proceed to GIFT only when previous IVF has at least demonstrated that the sperm are capable of fertilization.

What is POST?

Peritoneal oocyte and sperm transfer (POST) is an alternative treatment to GIFT, but it is possible to perform the operation under local anaesthesia. The eggs are recovered using ultrasound guidance, and the eggs and sperm are injected into the pelvis either via the vagina or abdomen. It is known that the fimbural ends of the fallopian tube are able to pick up the eggs and the sperm either swim into or are also 'picked up' by the tube. Fertilization thus occurs naturally within the tube (as with GIFT).

   As with IVF and GIFT, it is necessary to stimulate the ovaries to produce more than one egg and the procedure thus carries the inherent risk of a multiple pregnancy. The incidence of ectopic pregnancy is not unknown but is likely to be as high as with GIFT (plus or minus four per cent). Preliminary reports are encouraging showing a pregnancy rate of thirty to thirty-five per cent per treatment cycle.

What is DIPI?

Direct Intra Peritoneal Insemination (DIPI) is a modified form of artificial insemination using husbands' or donor semen. The sperm preparation is injected into the pelvis via the vagina under local anaesthesia. It has been used to overcome cervical mucus hostility and in some cases of male infertility. Preliminary reports show a pregnancy rate of ten to fourteen per cent per treatment cycle.

Guidelines of IVF Units

These will vary between units, but at St Mary's in Manchester we are only able to offer treatment to couples who have been living together for at least three years and who don't have a child resident with them by this or a previous relationship.

We can't accept couples in whom a 'male factor' is solely responsible for their childlessness, and we don't treat women aged forty or over, as the success rate in this age group is so low. We are also only able to accept couples who reside within the geographical boundaries covered by the North West Regional Health Authority.

If you are overweight it is difficult to see the ovaries on the scan. We would prefer to treat women who are close to the ideal body weight for their height.

17

Cervical Cancer Screening

J. Elizabeth Macgregor

This chapter is good news. It's about prevention. The object of screening is to prevent the development of invasive cancer, and because of the location of the uterine cervix, samples of cells may be easily and painlessly taken and examined under a microscope. If abnormalities are found they may be treated before they progress to cancer. This cannot easily be done for other organs like the lungs or stomach as none is so readily accessible as the cervix. This means that cervical cancer is the only cancer, at present, which can be prevented.

Cervical cancer is a sexually transmitted disease, and has been known to exist for over a century. With the exception of one extremely rare variety, it does not occur in nuns or women who have never had intercourse; and since it may pass from one sexual partner to another, women who have many partners are at greater risk of developing cervical cancer than those who have few. It is also suggested that women who have had intercourse from an early age are more liable to develop the disease than those whose sexual activities began later in life. All sexually active women should have regular cervical smears. Only the woman herself knows how active she is and so when she requires her first smear. The Family Planning Association doctors take cervical smears when a woman starts contraception – an indication that she is sexually active. Most GPs, but not all, prescribing contraception measures will also take smears.

In 1966 the British Government suggested screening women over thirty-five years, based on the observed pattern of mortality. Later, opportunistic screening was recommended for all women, including those under thirty-five years, when they attended for other forms of medical care, such as pregnancy and contraception. This led to some women being well screened and others not being screened at all. By 1984 the Government had realized the chaos this caused and recommended a programme of screening beginning at the age of twenty, with repeat smears every five years. This is the programme that exists today. There is no upper age limit, although it is generally accepted that a woman who has had regular smears throughout her life may stop at about sixty years, provided her last smear was about three years previously.

The genesis of cervical cancer is not known and is probably a combination of factors. Research work shows there is a strong possibility that the disease is caused by a virus (see chapter 18). When the virus is conclusively identified, prevention may well take a different form – like immunization or vaccination – but that is a long way off. Meanwhile, the cervical smear test serves the purpose.

Where to go

Most cervical smears are taken by family doctors. Many group practices have a woman doctor who will hold special sessions to do this. If for any reason your doctor doesn't provide this service, he will be able to tell you where it can be done locally, at the Family Planning Clinic, for example. In the first instance, however, consult your family doctor.

Having the Test

Once an appointment has been made there is very little to worry about. The test itself is obviously very personal and you may find it slightly uncomfortable, but it is generally painless.

First of all you will be asked some simple questions about your menstrual cycle and any pregnancies you may have had. Then you will be asked to remove your pants and lie on a couch, either on your back or on your side with your legs drawn up, so that the doctor can place a metal or plastic instrument (speculum) into your vagina, to enable him or her to see your cervix clearly. If you relax you will scarcely feel this, but if you tense up, your muscles tighten, and the whole exercise becomes more difficult for you both.

The doctor then uses a wooden or plastic spatula to obtain a sample of cells from your cervix. Once he has that, he removes the speculum and the test is complete.

What happens to the Cells he obtains?

The doctor will spread the cells he has collected with the spatula on to a glass slide. Your name and some form of identification, either your address or a number, will already be written on the end of the slide. This is essential to ensure that tests are never mixed up. He then applies a solution to 'fix' the sample, and the slide is ready to be taken or posted off to the laboratory.

What happens in the Laboratory?

The slides are 'booked in' when they arrive at the laboratory, that is they are entered in a book with your name and a number. In many cases this test will be linked to any previous smear tests you have had. A growing number of laboratories use computers for this.

The cells on the slide are stained, to distinguish the different parts of each, and examined under a microscope by highly trained technicians or doctors. All abnormal smears are checked by a doctor.

This interpretation of the cervical smear is time-consuming, and when many slides come into the laboratory at the same time (perhaps after a newspaper article or television programme on the subject, which greatly increases the work-load) there may be a delay in each slide being read. Usually, however, the report will be back to your doctor within a month from the time the laboratory received it.

Results of the Test

The results of a smear fall into roughly four categories. 1. Unsatisfactory. The rate of unsatisfactory smears varies between three per cent and seven per cent, and happens for a variety of reasons. It may be that the smear contains so much mucus and pus that they obscure the cells the doctor needs to see and on which he bases his report. Similarly, if you have recently finished a menstrual period, the smear may be contaminated with blood, and again difficult to read. On other occasions the smear may have an inadequate number of cells present. It can be too scanty to justify a result being given.

Unsatisfactory smears must be repeated. Don't be alarmed. There's no need to worry any more than you did when you had the original smear taken. Nevertheless, if you are asked to go back for a repeat test, it is wise to keep the appointment.

2. Inflammatory Conditions. Cells which show inflammatory changes are not indicative of severe abnormality. The changes are probably due to an infection, such as thrush, and can be treated easily by pills or pessaries. Sometimes your partner will be treated at the same time.

3. Atypical, Borderline, or Dyskaryotic. Cells have changed and they are exactly as the name describes them: slightly different from normal and the doctor does not know why. He will be cautious and you will be asked to have a repeat smear, perhaps in three months time. Very often this repeat smear will be all right. If it is more abnormal than the previous test, you will be given treatment.

4. 'Positive'. Positive smears show cell changes which the doctor considers might at some later date turn to cancer if they were left untreated. The fact that treatment is required, does *not* mean you have cancer. Cancer is being prevented. It is an amber light, a warning. If left untreated those positive cells might not turn into cancer for ten to fifteen years, although a very few cases may progress more rapidly. If they are treated, however, they will not become cancer.

When you are told you have a 'positive' smear you will be given an appointment to see a consultant gynaecologist. There is no need to panic; treatment is simple and virtually painless.

Treatment

Treatment is usually carried out in the out-patient department of a hospital. Once upon a time this would have been impossible, but thanks to the introduction, in the last ten years, of an instrument called a colposcope, these operations can be done on the spot. A colposcope is a kind of microscope through which the consultant gynaecologist can look at the cervix, just as was done when you had the smear taken, but this time under magnification. This enables him to pin-point the abnormal area of the cervix and take from it a small piece of tissue. Again this is almost painless and you can go home immediately afterwards; to return about two weeks later. This is discussed in detail in chapter 18.

The tissue in the meantime will go to the tissue laboratory where a specialist doctor can decide how extensive and how deep the abnormal tissue is. The treatment that follows depends on his diagnosis. If you want a name for this condition (which is not cancer), it is cervical intrepithelial neoplasia (CIN).

CIN occurs in three grades, 1, 2 and 3. Grade 3 is the most severe, but even grade 3 is easily treated, and it is still not cancer. When you go back to see the gynaecologist, he will know which grade of CIN you have and will remove the abnormal tissue. In most cases this can be done in the out-patient department once again, without anaesthetic, and it is almost painless. If you are very nervous, of course, anaesthetics are to hand.

Once treatment is completed you should go back to having regular smears. You may be asked – allowed – to have them annually, as they do in the USA. Unfortunately, this is a 'luxury' in this country, but a woman who has had treatment deserves this extra care to ensure that cancer never develops.

Frequency of Tests

One of the problems in deciding whom and how often to screen is the lack of knowledge of how long the disease takes to develop. Prospective studies to see how long it takes for a lesion detected by a cervical smear to progress to invasive disease is not ethically possible: a woman who has a positive smear must be treated.

Retrospective studies indicate that in the majority of cases invasive cervical cancer is slow in developing. Once abnormal cells are found it may be many years before invasion occurs. Research has shown that where there is comprehensive coverage by screening of the female population, such as in the north-east of Scotland, in Iceland, in Scandinavian countries and in British Columbia, there is a fall in the incidence of the disease. Regular screening, therefore, is effective in preventing cervical cancer.

Studies on the amount of protection a woman receives when she has had a cervical smear have recently been carried out in the north-east of Scotland, where it was found that a woman has a high degree of protection in the first two years after a negative smear. The degree of protection then falls steadily as time elapses, but even after ten years there is a degree of protection still apparent when compared to a woman who has never had a smear at all.

A recent collaborative study under the auspices of the World Health Organization was organized by Dr N. E. Day to evaluate cervical cancer screening programmes in eight countries with very different policies. The protection given by a smear was found to be higher in women who had had two or more negative smears than in women who had only had one. There was little difference between screening every year or every three years, but if screening was repeated at five- or ten-yearly intervals the protection was considerably less.

This study group also found that centrally well-organized programmes were more effective than uncoordinated opportunistic screening programmes. Comprehensive coverage of the population is as important as the frequency of screening. The more frequently women have smear tests, the lower the incidence of the disease will become, but the greater the cost to the nation. It is this balance between cost and effectiveness that has to be considered; and at present the Government guidelines are for five-yearly tests, but this is under review, and it is possible that a three-yearly interval will be recommended.

All the evidence from international sources suggests that comprehensive coverage of the women at risk will reduce the incidence of the disease by as much as ninety per cent. At present many of the women who die from cancer of the cervix every year regrettably will never have had a smear test, or will have been poorly screened. The arguments for having the test regularly are irrefutable.

18
Pre-Cancer of the Cervix – Causes and Treatment

Albert Singer

What is Cervical Cancer?

The cervix, like all tissues of the body, is made up of cells which resemble minute building blocks. Cancer is a disease of these cells. Although cells in every part of the body may appear to look and work differently, most repair and reproduce themselves in the same way. Normally this process takes place in an orderly and controlled manner, but in some cases the process gets out of control, the cells continue to multiply and eventually develop into a lump, known as a tumour, which can be either benign or malignant.

In the benign tumour the cells do not spread to other parts of the body and so are not cancerous. If they continue to grow from the site of origin, however, they may cause a problem by pressing on and invading surrounding organs.

A malignant tumour is made up of cells which do have the ability to spread beyond their site of origin and obviously if left untreated will invade and destroy the surrounding tissues. Occasionally these cells break away from the original lump, or what is called the primary cancer, and spread to other organs in the body by the bloodstream or lymphatic systems. When they reach these sites they may continue the process of dividing and multiplying and form a completely new tumour. This is then called a secondary or metastic tumour.

When a tumour develops, a sample can be taken and examination of the small sample of cells under a microscope would tell whether the tumour is benign or malignant. It is important to realize that cancer is not a single disease with a single cause and with a single type of treatment. There are at least 200 different types of cancer which each have their own name and treatment.

The Cervix

Structure
The cervix is the lowest part of the uterus and is often called the neck of the womb. It is a muscular pear-shaped organ at the top of the vagina, and its skin or lining, is continuous with that of the uterus above and the vaginal passage below. The cervix can easily be seen during an internal vaginal examination by the use of a metal speculum.

The cervix is drained by a collection of lymph nodes or glands, which are sited close by in the pelvic area. These, each one about the size of a bean, allow colourless fluid, or lymph, to pass through and act primarily as a defence system against disease. These lymph glands are an important drainage system for cancer and with malignant disease they are affected at an early stage.

Pre-Cancers
The cervix is most unusual in that it is one of the few internal organs whose cancer has a definite pre-cancerous stage. As explained in chapter 17 this stage is divided into three types. They range from the very mild, CIN 1, to the more advanced, CIN 3. If left, CIN 3 will progress to cancer of the cervix in about one third of cases. To date, however, there is no way of telling which CIN changes will progress on to cancer. It seems from research so far that CIN 1 may have the potential to progress to the CIN 3 stage; therefore we regard all of these changes (i.e. CIN) as potentially malignant.

The difficulty is that these changes are completely silent, in that there are no symptoms from them. They do not cause abnormal bleeding or discharge and on looking at the cervix there is very little that seems amiss. They can only be detected by the smear test and then by observing the cervix through a magnifying apparatus called a colposcope (see p. 133). If they are found at this early stage, these pre-cancerous changes are a hundred per cent curable. Once they have started to spread, they are more difficult to cure. However, even at the first stage of the malignant change, (i.e. after they have progressed from a pre-cancerous to a cancerous stage) they still have an eighty per cent chance of being cured.

The Cause

An increasing problem
Within the last five years there seems to have been a dramatic
increase in this disease. Normally, in its pre-cancerous form, it
would affect approximately twenty women in every thousand,
but within the last few years this rate has trebled. This is
especially so in women under the age of thirty. About two
thousand women per year die from this cancer in Britain and
every one of those could have been avoided, because if it had
been detected in its pre-cancerous stage, it could have been
treated and cured.

Behavioural causes of the disease
It has been known for over a hundred and fifty years that the
most common form of the cervical cancer and its pre-cancer, i.e.
the squamous, or flat-skinned, type of cancer, which occurs in
about ninety-five per cent of women with the disease, is related to
sexual intercourse. As far as it is known, there has never been a
report of a virginal woman contracting either the cancer or the
pre-cancer of the squamous type, although they can suffer from
the more rare type, the so-called gland or adeno cancer. Thus it
would seem that some substance passed during intercourse is
related to the origins of the disease.
    It is also well known that certain patterns of behaviour put
some women more at risk than others. Women who marry
young, and therefore first have intercourse at an early age, have
been found to be particularly prone. Frequently, early intercourse and marriage also leads to an increased number of sexual
partners, which is significant. However, it must be stressed, and
stressed firmly, that many women who have had only one sexual
partner and who marry late in life can also contract the disease.
Not surprisingly, women who develop other sexually transmitted diseases have a high incidence of this disease; so do
women who are infertile. It is also well known that women who
are widowed, or who have unstable marriages, who are divorced
or separated from their husbands, are also at increased risk.
    The ethnic group and social class of the woman also seems to be
a factor. In the USA women who are of Puerto Rican or Spanish
origin have a rate three to four times that of their white sisters,
and black women have a rate slightly lower than either. On the
other hand, we know that women who belong to orthodox
religious groups, such as Seventh Day Adventists, Muslims,
Jews and the rather select Amish Group, have very low occur-

rence of the disease. It is also known that women who live in rural areas have less disease than those who live in urban areas, and women confined to prison seem to have one of the highest rates known. However, it is becoming more common to find women with the disease who have none of these characteristics and the emphasis has now shifted. Where the woman has been monogamous or has had very few sexual partners, we have started to concentrate on the sexual behaviour of the male. It seems as though his sexual behaviour, particularly if he began having intercourse at an early age and has had multiple partners, puts his partner at risk of contracting cervical cancer.

What are the 'agents' involved?
By agents, one means the causative factor, and there are two types: one can be related to a virus or a bacteria spread during intercourse; the second to the actual sperm, or male gamete, itself.

Women who attend sexually transmitted disease clinics have a high rate of cervical cancer. They also have a number of bacterial organisms, such as thrush (Monilia) and Trichomonas and more recently Chlamydia or cytomegalovirus. There is no evidence, however, to suggest that any of these are responsible for the cervical cancer. It would seem much more likely that it is a virus which gets into the cell and causes mischief than one of these simple bacterium.

The viruses that seem to be most incriminated are those of the *herpes genitalis* type, or the human papilloma or wart virus. Fifteen years ago it was thought that the herpes virus, which is very common, was the cause of cervical cancer. This was because the antibodies against the herpes virus were found in the blood of many women suffering from cervical cancer. However, it has now been proven that many women, who have neither the cancer nor pre-cancer, possess this antibody and its presence is probably no more than a reflection of sexual behaviour. The most telling point is that the genetic fragment of the herpes virus cannot be isolated from the actual cancer itself. As you will see below, this is a common feature of the wart virus.

The human papillomavirus, or wart virus, is commonly found in the genital tract of both men and women. In its simplest form it causes warts in many parts of the body and on the genitals. There seem to be about forty-two different types of this virus, the most serious being the 16 and 18 variety. Simple genital warts found on the penis in the man or the vulva of a woman are usually type 6 and 11, but the pre-cancers and cancers contain the more serious type 16 and 18. In the actual cancer, approximately seventy to ninety per cent of women have the genetic fragment of the wart virus in the cancer. It seems to have interlocked itself into the genetic material of the cell and therefore tends to direct the growth processes. What is worrying is that in the pre-cancers, fragments of type 16 and 18 are also found in about fifty to seventy-five per cent of cases. In these, the virus is outside the actual genetic machinery in what is called an *episomal* form.

Recent work has also shown that many cancers of the cervix treated nearly half a century ago have fragments of the wart virus within them. Also studies conducted fifteen years ago on large populations seem to show that the virus was very common, even at that time, but was unrecognized. Most exciting are the experiments from Philadelphia, where fragments of the wart virus have been inserted into cells of mice whose immunity system has been removed. In about sixty per cent of the tissue implanted into a mouse, a pre-cancerous state developed following infection with the virus.

It seems as though the infection is not only common in women but also in men. Recent evidence suggests that men can carry a virus not only in the form of obvious warts on their penis, but also in a previously hidden form that can only be detected with the use of a magnifying glass. It is now well accepted, however, that if a man has penile warts then the chances of his partner developing cervical cancer are roughly between twenty and thirty per cent. This undiagnosed form of the disease is still a matter of controversy and one does not know how infectious these changes are. So far it would only be advisable to recommend the screening of the male partner if he has obvious penile or other genital warts. It is not recommended that all male partners of women with cervical pre-cancer or cancer come along for examination.

Diagnosis and Treatment

Cervical pre-cancer can be easily detected by the cervical smear (see chapter 17). Once the smear is accepted as abnormal, no matter how abnormal, then the woman should be sent for colposcopic examination. This involves looking at the cervix with the use of a strong light and a microscope, and is completely painless. A biopsy is usually taken from the cervix where the abnormal change is present. If pre-cancer is diagnosed on the biopsy specimen and all of the abnormal change can be seen through the colposcope then the woman can either be treated with a freezing technique (cryosurgery), or as is more common nowadays, with the laser. These treatments are in themselves painless and cause very little inconvenience; they are also highly effective, with nearly a ninety-five per cent cure after one treatment. Recurrence of the disease can be treated with further treatments.

If, however, at colposcopy there is a suspicion of an early cancer, or the surgeon is unhappy about being able to see all of the abnormal change, then he or she may remove part of the cervix by a simple operation called a cone biopsy, which is usually performed under general anaesthesia. Even if there is very early invasive cancer present, this cone biopsy can sometimes remove the disease completely, with nearly a hundred per cent chance of complete cure.

The laser machine offers the possibility of treating pre-cancers in other parts of the genital tract as well. It is now common to find pre-cancers normally associated with the cervix, in the vagina and the vulva. These can also be cured in most cases with one application of laser with very little damage to the tissues; and there is no damage or interference in any way with any of the laser treatments to the woman's chances of future pregnancy.

The Future

Cervical pre-cancer and cancer will continue to rise over the next decade. Unless there is a dramatic change in sexual behaviour then this disease will continue to take its toll. With the increasing public awareness of AIDS there is a possibility that sexual behaviour will change and in turn this will affect the incidence of cervical disease. The tragedy is that cervical cancer should not kill a single woman. It is eminently preventable.

19
Operations for the Treatment of Women's Cancer

John M. Monaghan

Cervical Cancer

Cancer of the cervix, or 'neck of the womb', remains one of the most common cancers to occur in women. However, if symptoms are reported to your doctor early, in most cases the cancer can be cured.

The cervix is that part of the uterus which protrudes into the upper part of the vagina (fig. 1). It is mainly covered by skin similar to that of the outer part of the body, but also has some skin which secretes the natural mucus (discharge) which all women experience. The fact that it has these two different types of skin means that two different types of cancer can develop. They each produce similar symptoms and are managed in similar ways.

Cancer of the cervix we know develops from a pre-cancerous condition known as CIN, which can be readily diagnosed using cervical smears (see chapter 17). The change from pre-cancer to cancer is one which is often poorly understood. In a nut-shell, the difference between these two conditions is that the pre-cancer is entirely confined to the surface layers of skin on the cervix, whereas the fully developed cancer has invaded the tissues below the skin surface, and has already developed a tendency to spread by the drainage channels (lymphatics) of the cervix out towards the side of the pelvis.

Symptoms and signs
This cancer can occur at any age between twenty and ninety, but

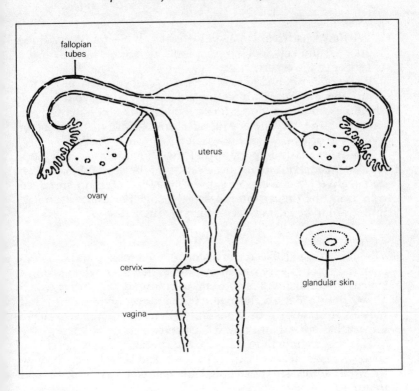

it is most common in women who are still menstruating between the ages of forty and fifty. An alarming increase has recently been noted in younger age groups.

Bleeding is the most common symptom and may show itself as altered periods (usually heavier or irregular), or as bleeding between periods, particularly after intercourse when the delicate blood vessels of the cancer may be damaged. Discharge often occurs at the same time and may be blood-stained and/or smell offensive, due to infection in the surface of the cancer.

Pain is not usually associated with early stages of the cancer. It tends to occur in later stages of the disease due to pressure or spread of the cancer to the nerves of the pelvis, which causes back and leg pain rather like sciatica. It is important, however, to remember that most people with backache do not have cancer. Listlessness and tiredness may be produced by the bleeding and the infection.

Methods of diagnosis
If you have had regular negative cervical smears (every three years), it is unlikely that the symptoms mentioned above are due to cancer of the cervix.

If you have not had regular screening and you have any of the symptoms mentioned above you should go and see your GP. He should examine you and if he is suspicious that you may have a cancer of the cervix he will refer you to a gynaecologist or gynaecological oncologist (a women's cancer specialist).

It is particularly important that the GP should not rely on a single smear result to diagnose cancer of the cervix. Smears can be negative when a cancer is present as the infection and dead cells from the cancer can mask the result. For this reason it is important to have smear tests taken regularly.

AT THE HOSPITAL
The specialist will take a brief history of the problem and will then examine you in a very similar manner to that used when taking a smear. He or she will also examine you with his fingers which allows him to identify the extent of the cancer on the cervix, and may also examine the back passage to determine if there has been any further spread away from the cervix.

This first examination will give the specialist a very good idea as to whether there is a cancer present, and he will then arrange for your admission to hospital for complete assessment and treatment.

In the hospital, blood will be taken for testing, your chest and kidneys will be X-rayed, and an anaesthetist will visit you to make sure you are fit for the examination under anaesthetic.

EXAMINATION UNDER ANAESTHETIC
Once you have been transferred from your ward to the operating theatre and anaesthetized, which is now commonly done by a simple injection in the back of the hand, the surgeon will examine you once again as he or she did in the out-patient department in order to determine the full extent of the cancer. This is called 'staging'.He will also look into the bladder and remove a sample of the area suspected to be cancerous so that it can be looked at under a microscope.

When you return from theatre you may have a pack in the vagina and possibly a catheter (small tube) in the bladder, both of which are removed twenty-four hours later. The doctors will come and see you and explain what they have found and how they plan to manage the cancer. Then if there is no further bleeding you will be allowed to go home. Occasionally, if there is some doubt about the diagnosis, you may have to await the results of the microscopic examination before knowing what treatment the specialist plans.

The treatment of cancer is so complex that you may well be referred to yet another specialist at this stage, either a gynaecological oncologist or a radiotherapist.

In general, if you are under forty-five years of age and the cancer is small, you will be offered an operation to clear the disease. If you are older, or the cancer is more extensive, then radiotherapy may be chosen as the best option. The choice of procedure varies from one part of the country to another, and you should ask the doctor to explain why he is choosing a particular method of treatment.

The operation – radical hysterectomy
If you are offered an operation as the method of treatment this usually means a radical hysterectomy. This operation differs from an ordinary hysterectomy in that it is more extensive and complex to perform, therefore there are fewer doctors with the necessary skill. You may have to be referred to a centre where they carry out a lot of these operations.

In a radical hysterectomy the whole uterus (womb) is removed, together with the cervix and the cancer. In order to be sure that the cancer is cleared, a wide band of normal tissue must also be taken away, which means you lose the top half of the vagina too, plus the tissue stretching out to the bony part of the pelvis. To treat any possible spread, the glands on the side wall of the pelvis are also removed and sent for examination.

In some major centres, before embarking on a radical hysterectomy, the surgeon removes the glands further up the back of the abdomen, and they are looked at straight away under the microscope. If they show no evidence that the cancer has spread, the operation is carried out as planned. If, however, they show that the cancer has spread to these glands, then the treatment must be modified. This may mean performing the radical hysterectomy and then treating you with chemotherapy (drug treatment) after the operation, or stopping the operation, and once the wounds have healed, treating you with a combination of radiotherapy and chemotherapy instead.

In younger women (under forty-five years), the ovaries can be kept so that although the periods will stop, your hormones will continue to be produced so you will not have any symptoms of the change of life (menopause).

The scar left by a radical hysterectomy will run up and down the lower part of the abdomen. This is so that the surgeon can easily reach all the parts of the pelvis which need to be treated. A transverse (bikini) incision is not adequate and makes the operation unnecessarily difficult.

Back in the ward you will have a drip in your arm which will stay in place for the first few days after the operation. There will also be a catheter in the bladder to rest it for five days or so. This catheter may be inserted from below, but nowadays it is more common to put it into the bladder through the lower abdominal wall, which allows the urine to flow spontaneously when the bladder is fully rested. Frequently, small tubes are also brought out through the abdominal wall and connected to bottles. These are to drain excess fluid from within the abdomen.

If it seems that an excessive number of tubes are attached to you, you must remember that they all speed recovery and are rapidly removed in the first few post-operative days.

Getting out of bed is encouraged from the first day after the operation. It is important to move a lot, even though it may be painful at first. Early movement cuts down the risk of thrombosis (clots) developing in the legs, and more dangerously, in the lungs.

The stay in hospital is usually ten days, but this will depend very much on how fast your recovery is.

FURTHER TREATMENT

What happens next will depend on the results of the microscopical examination of the tissues removed. If there has been no spread of the cancer into the glands at the side of the pelvis, then no further treatment is necessary.

If, however, the glands have been shown to contain some cancer cells, then further treatment following the operation is essential. This will either take the form of radiotherapy to the pelvis, or chemotherapy (drug treatment). Occasionally the two will be combined; but either way, the specialist will explain why he is recommending this extra treatment and why he has made his choice.

RECOVERY

How well and how quickly you recover after you go home depends to a great extent upon your attitude. It is vitally important that you do not take to your bed. Old-fashioned ideas of taking months to recover are unnecessary, and indeed dangerous. A good diet and steadily increasing exercise are essential to a full and successful recovery.

You will be seen again by the specialist six weeks after the operation, and then regularly for many years thereafter.

SIDE EFFECTS
Many patients do suffer side effects from radical hysterectomy. The most common is difficulty in passing urine; in particular the feeling of wanting to pass urine is lost, or reduced, and you have to 'push' in order to empty the bladder properly. This problem may last for many months, but in almost all cases returns to normal. Your urine may also become infected immediately after the operation, in which case you will need antibiotic treatment to clear it up, prescribed either by the hospital doctors or your own GP.

One of the major worries for many women, however, is how the operation will affect their sexual relationship with their partners. I usually advise patients not to have intercourse for six weeks, which is usually the time at which you are reviewed in the clinic. Many patients are distressed to discover on the first attempt at intercourse that the vagina is markedly shorter than it was. If you have not had radiotherapy, and you have intercourse regularly and gently, the vagina will rapidly lengthen to close to its original size. Unfortunately, if you have had radiotherapy, this recovery frequently does not occur and a degree of shrinkage and dryness has to be accepted. In any event, you need have no fear that having intercourse will in any way provoke a return of the cancer.

Alternative medicine
Despite its promise of natural treatment and cures, alternative medicine has never been shown to be effective in treating cancer. Orthodox medical methods are the only really effective means of treatment and cure.

It must be understood, however, that many failures of treatment do occur and the risk of failure is higher, the further the disease has progressed by the time it is diagnosed.

People frequently turn to alternative medicine when the disease recurs, but the most you can expect from these methods is that you will be put on to a good diet and have the care and attention of dedicated individuals. Perhaps this caring approach should be widely available in the National Health Service. Unfortunately, it is not.

Cancer of the Ovary

Cancer of the ovary is a very difficult disease to diagnose in its early stages because at the moment there are no reliable screening tests. The cancer grows relatively silently within the pelvis and abdomen, without the patient noting any major alterations in health. It is frequently found that the diagnosis is not made until the cancer has grown to a very large size or even spread widely, thus making cure difficult.

Symptoms
The symptoms which occur in ovarian cancer are frequently vague: bowel upsets, indigestion, pelvic discomfort, menstrual upsets, backache, feelings of pressure, dragging sensations and even breathlessness all have been described.

Most cancers of the ovary develop in the form of cysts producing large fluid-filled spaces which expand steadily within the abdomen. Any symptoms which occur develop because the cancer presses on structures close to it. These will include the bladder, producing feelings of wanting to pass urine, or causing you to pass frequent small quantities of urine. At its worst this pressure may make it difficult for you to control the urine and leakage may occur.

The bowel may also be affected, causing a desire to empty the bowel but with little result or alternatively with constipation or diarrhoea if the cancer irritates the bowel.

As the cancer grows, you may notice your waist size increasing without any real increase in weight.

This swelling of the abdomen may not only be due to the growth of the cysts, but also to the collection of large quantities of fluid (ascites), which can cause the swelling to become enormous.

Bleeding, pain, discharge and sweats are also symptoms of this cancer, but not very common.

Methods of diagnosis
As with cancer of the body of the uterus, it is easy to be lulled into a false sense of security by having a cervical smear test and receiving a negative, or normal, result. Only very rarely does the cervical smear test pick up evidence of this cancer. It is important, therefore, that your GP takes your symptoms seriously and refers you for a specialist gynaecological opinion. One of the most common errors made in this disease is that you are sent to the wrong specialist, who may spend a considerable time making the correct diagnosis.

At the hospital the vagina, abdomen and the neck of the womb will all be examined fully. The specialist is feeling for cysts in the abdomen and glands in the neck. If you have a large cyst in the abdomen the specialist will be able to make a confident diagnosis that you have a cyst of the ovary; unfortunately, however, it is impossible at this stage to be certain that the tumour is cancerous. If there is some doubt about the presence of a cyst the specialist may ask for an ultrasound scan of the abdomen and pelvis, which will clearly show if there is one and may also give clear guidance to the specialist as to the likelihood of it being a cancer. The test is easily performed and is quite painless, (see chapter 6).

If a cyst is found you will be admitted to hospital as soon as possible for an operation called a laparotomy. This means 'opening of the abdomen' and is deliberately vague because the specialist wishes to be able to deal with whatever he finds inside.

The operation
The laparotomy consists of removing all cancer which is present in the abdomen. This is important as the operation is only part of the treatment and has to be complemented by the use of chemotherapy (drug treatment) to deal with any microscopic cancer cells which may have been left behind. The drug treatment will work best if the surgeon does not leave any visible tumour behind. The operation itself is not complicated but it means removing both ovaries, the uterus, the tubes and the omentum (a piece of tissue from higher up in the abdomen) and any small particles of cancer which may lie on other organs.

You may be surprised that so much will be removed when the cancer is only affecting the ovary. The reason for this extensive operation is that even though the cancer may only be in one ovary there is a high risk of it already being in the other ovary even though it may not yet be visible and a risk of it spreading to the womb as well. The omentum is also removed because it too is at high risk of being affected by the spreading cancer.

Back in the ward, you will have a drip in your arm which will stay in place for the first few days after the operation. In this procedure it is rare to have tubes coming from the abdomen to suction bottles for drainage. Occasionally a catheter is inserted into the bladder either from below or through the abdominal wall.

Once again getting out of bed is encouraged from the first day after the operation to cut down the risk of the development of thrombosis (clots) in the legs and more dangerously in the lungs.

The drug treatment has to be carefully checked, so regular

blood tests will be carried out before each course of treatment and you will have either ultrasound or Computerized Axial Tomography (known as a body or CAT scan) examinations at intervals to keep an eye on how you are doing.

RECOVERY
Although recovery from the operation is rapid, many of the drug treatments have a tendency to make you feel sick and low. This effect wears off rapidly after each treatment, but as you usually have five or six courses it is likely that you will feel unwell at intervals over a period of six months or so.

SIDE EFFECTS
Side effects of the operation itself are very few. Sometimes the urine becomes infected and you may need to have an antibiotic. Occasionally the wound leaks for a while but this always settles down.

The most serious side effects occur during your drug treatment and this is why you are so carefully monitored at this time. As well as damaging the cancer cells, some drugs also damage the blood cells. Regular blood tests are taken therefore and if they reveal damage, the treatment will be stopped for two to three weeks to give your blood time to recover. From a physical point of view the vagina will return to normal within about six weeks of the operation and a sexual relationship is possible at this stage. Mentally, however, this cancer is very demanding as the treatment takes a long time and you will not feel a hundred per cent until the drug treatment is complete. It is not unusual to feel tired, irritable and depressed, and you also may find you have no appetite or enjoyment of food. This period of time calls for a lot of understanding from both partners.

Cancer of the Body of the Uterus

It may seem difficult to understand why there should be a different cancer occurring in the main part of the womb from that occurring in the neck of the womb. The main reason for this is that the tissues from which each of these cancers develops are basically different.

The cancer of the body or main part of the uterus also has different characteristics from cervical cancer in that it generally occurs in women after the periods have naturally stopped (after the menopause), although it can also occur in younger women. It is usually a cancer of the glandular tissue in the lining of the body of the uterus, but there are also some rarer cancers of the muscular part of the womb.

Symptoms
As the cancer tends to develop after the menopause the most important symptom is that of bleeding beginning again. The temptation to say 'It's just my age' is enormous; however, all bleeding from the vagina after the periods have apparently stopped should be thoroughly investigated. Very few other symptoms occur so it is doubly important not to ignore this bleeding. For the woman who is still menstruating a major alteration in menstrual pattern should also be taken seriously and fully investigated. Pelvic discomfort, backache, feelings of pressure and dragging sensations may be felt, but these symptoms are not specific for this disease.

It is important therefore that you take your symptoms to a GP and that he or she refers you for a specialist gynaecological opinion. This will almost certainly be followed by admission to hospital for tests.

ADMISSION TO HOSPITAL
This is necessary because during out-patient pelvic examinations the specialist can get a clear view of the vagina and the neck of the womb but is unable to say what is happening within the cavity of the womb. He will therefore want to perform a diagnostic curettage, (D & C). This procedure is carried out under a short general anaesthetic and consists of scraping samples of the lining of the womb and sending them for analysis under the microscope by the pathologist.

Occasionally the specialist does not find any scrapings because the cancer is so small and he will then inform you of this result and discharge you from the hospital. Sometimes the bleeding which first brought you to the hospital returns. Do not ignore it; report it to your doctor who should then refer you back to the specialist again. The specialist should again perform a D & C.

The scraping which the specialist took is sent for microscopical examination and the result is usually available in about a week. If the scraping shows evidence of a cancer of the body of the womb you will be recalled and the specialist will tell you that it is necessary to have further treatment. This will probably be a form of hysterectomy.

THE OPERATION

The specialist will arrange for you to be admitted to hospital within the next few weeks. You will go in on the day before the operation so that a small series of blood tests can be performed and you will be examined and seen by the anaesthetist.

As with cancer of the cervix you will probably have a vertical incision because this allows the surgeon better access. Occasionally, however, this operation is performed through a transverse or 'bikini' incision.

Back in the ward you will have a drip in your arm which will stay in place for the first few days; and as with the other operations, getting out of bed is encouraged from the first day after the operation. How long you stay in hospital will depend very much on how fast your recovery is, but it is usually eight to ten days.

FURTHER TREATMENT

This will depend on the results of the microscopical examination of the tissues removed. If the cancer has begun to grow deeper into the muscle wall of the uterus, or is of a type which has a tendency to spread, your specialist may recommend that your surgical treatment is boosted with a course of radiotherapy to the lower abdomen. Some specialists also recommend that you take a form of hormone treatment (chemotherapy), which may have an action against the cancer as well.

It is important, however, to remember that both radiotherapy and chemotherapy are usually only used after surgery and are not as effective by themselves.

RECOVERY

This will be dependent on your age and physical state before the operation. It is important to move about as much as possible once you get home and steadily and progressively to increase your movement. This is particularly important if you are overweight, as many patients who have this disease tend to be.

SIDE EFFECTS

These are mainly confined to the pre-menopausal woman due to the effects of losing her ovaries. The removal of the ovaries can produce sudden severe menopausal symptoms of hot flushes, sleeplessness, irritability, depression and tearfulness or even suicidal feelings. In the first few months after the operation these symptoms can be helped, but not effectively cleared because the only way to do so would be to use hormone replacement therapy

(HRT), which is inadvisable after this cancer. If the symptoms persist for more than a year and there has been no evidence of a recurrence of the cancer it is now thought that HRT can be given to treat very troublesome menopausal symptoms. (See chapter 23)

Your sexual relationship will be affected for several weeks and you will have some discomfort for some time after the operation but gradually with sympathy on both sides, it will recover.

Cancer of the Vulva

Cancer of the vulva (the skin or lips on the outer part of the vagina), is mainly a disease of older women, most of whom are in their sixties or seventies, but it can occur occasionally in very much younger women, even as young as those in their twenties and thirties.

It is a rare cancer but appears to be associated with other cancers and pre-cancers of the female organs particularly of the cervix (neck of the womb). The cause is not known.

Symptoms
The most important symptom associated with this cancer is irritation, soreness and itchiness of the vulva which may have been going on for years before the cancer actually develops.

This is the main reason why so many women delay consulting their doctor even when the cancer develops. Many patients treat themselves with creams and lotions which are obtained from the chemist. Unfortunately, it is also true that a number of doctors do not examine their patients correctly before prescribing creams. The patient then continues to receive the cream on a 'repeat prescription' basis and is not examined for a considerable length of time; the cancer meanwhile continues to grow.

A lump or mass is the second most common symptom and should be reported immediately to the doctor who should examine you properly. Pain does not occur in the early stages of the disease except for soreness and discomfort occurring in the small cuts and cracks which can develop in the itchy skin; but as the cancer grows bigger you will find it uncomfortable to sit down.

Bleeding is also rare in the early stages, but will occur as the tumour grows. The cancer also becomes infected and produces an offensive smell, which is made worse because of difficulties of keeping the area clean when opening the bowels or passing water.

Methods of diagnosis

The cancer of the vulva usually grows on the outside skin or lips
of the vulva and is thus easily seen when the doctor examines
you. It is obviously important that you should overcome any
nervousness or shyness you may feel and be examined correctly.
If your doctor has any suspicion that you may have a cancer he or
she will refer you for a specialist gynaecological opinion.

Management of this type of cancer will probably involve rather
a large operation, but before this the specialist will want to
confirm the diagnosis and will arrange for you to be admitted to
hospital for a small sample (a biopsy) of the cancer to be removed
and inspected under the microscope.

The operation

The taking of a biopsy is a simple procedure. You will be given a
brief anaesthetic and a small sample of the cancer will be removed
and sent for examination. Usually this result takes a few days to
return and the specialist will then inform you of the result. If the
cancer is confirmed you will be told that you require a much more
extensive and complicated operation, which has an excellent
chance of curing the problem. At this point the specialist will
usually recommend that you be referred to a cancer specialist (a
gynaecological oncologist), who has more experience of handling
this rare cancer. For older patients the prospect of having to travel
long distances to see another doctor may be hard to understand,
but there is little doubt that if you can be treated by a gynaecological oncologist your prospects for cure are very much better.

The operation is large because it is important that not only the
cancer on the skin of the vulva be removed but also the glands
(lymph nodes) in the groin on either side. This large operation
has been shown to be very much superior in cure rates when
compared to the lesser procedure of simply removing the cancer
on the vulva. The operation is now modified slightly in some
centres by carrying it out through three separate incisions, one in
each groin and the third around the cancer on the vulva. This
method should only be used for very small cancers. The scar is
known as a 'butterfly incision' for obvious reasons.

When you have been admitted for the main operation you will
be seen by the anaesthetist, who will explain to you the type of
anaesthetic which may be used. One of the best types is the
epidural anaesthetic (see chapter 11) which assists the surgeon
during the operation and also reduces the amount of anaesthetic
material that you will have to be given.

Back in the ward you will have a drip in your arm which will stay in place for the first few days after the operation. You will also have drainage tubes in each groin to remove excess fluid from the wounds. A catheter will also be in place in the bladder. These tubes will all be progressively removed in the days following operation. Once again, getting out of bed is encouraged from the second day after the operation; and the stay in hospital, usually fifteen to twenty-six days, will depend very much on how fast your recovery is.

FURTHER TREATMENT
This will depend on the results of the microscopical examination of the tissues removed. Occasionally it is thought necessary to apply radiotherapy to the groin area to add to the surgical treatment.

RECOVERY
This is usually excellent after this operation. For a time, while in the ward, walking may be rather slow, but this will return completely to normal before you go home.

SIDE EFFECTS
The most common problem that can occur is for the wounds in the groins to become infected and to separate. This may seem a disastrous occurrence to you at the time, but its major effect is to slow down your healing and delay you going home; it is not a life-threatening situation.

It is very important for you to be regularly followed up for the remainder of your life as there is a small risk of the cancer returning particularly on the vulva. If the cancer does recur it can be readily treated by another small operation.

Cancer of the Vagina

Cancer of the vagina is rare, it appears mainly in women in their sixties, but it has been known to occur occasionally in women of all ages, even small children and teenagers.

Symptoms
This cancer grows in the surface skin in the vagina and is often first noticed as unusual bleeding or discharge, both of which should be taken seriously and fully investigated. Pelvic discomfort, backache, feelings of pressure and dragging sensations are all possible, but not specific symptoms of this disease.

Methods of diagnosis

The cervical smear test only rarely picks up evidence of cancer of the vagina. Even when the cancer has grown to a significant size it can be missed despite an internal examination. This is because unless the doctor is particularly careful he may cover the cancer with the speculum which he has inserted. Your GP should take your symptoms seriously and refer you for a specialist gynaecological opinion.

At the hospital you will be seen first of all as an out-patient and will be asked a few questions about your problem. It is helpful if you can have the dates of your last period handy and a record of any unusual bleeding. A doctor will then examine you, in much the same way as he or she would if taking a cervical smear. The doctor will also use his fingers to feel the size of the cancer and if there is any evidence of spread.

After this you will be admitted to hospital for a full examination under anaesthetic, when a sample (biopsy) from the cancer will be taken for examination under the microscope.

The operation

The operation, called 'an examination under anaesthetic and biopsy of vagina', is usually combined with inspection of the bladder and the bowel.

A small sample of tissue from these areas is removed and sent to the pathologist for examination under the microscope. At the end of the operation a pack may be put into the vagina and a catheter into the bladder, both of which are usually removed on the morning after the operation. This examination of the tissue is extremely important as it forms the basis on which decisions are made as to the best method of treating your particular cancer. There are many different methods. The most common is a form of radiotherapy which uses external beams together with an internal treatment. A instrument containing radioactive material is inserted into the vagina and the length of time that the instrument remains inside is very carefully calculated so that the cancer is effectively treated without damaging the normal tissue around.

Recovery from the biopsy is very rapid, but recovery from the radiation treatment is usually slow, often because of bowel side effects, such as diarrhoea. Others, which came later, include bleeding from the bowel and severe shrinkage and dryness of the vagina.

Unfortunately, both surgical and radiotherapeutic treatment of cancer of the vagina will result in damage to or removal of the vagina, and obviously this will seriously affect your ability to have intercourse. It is possible to replace the vagina with a skin graft and this is something you should discuss with the doctor.

20
Chronic Pelvic Pain Due to Congestion

Richard W. Beard

What is Pelvic Pain?

Pelvic pain has been recognized for at least a hundred and fifty years as a condition that occurs uniquely in women of child-bearing age. The medical literature of all Western countries has numerous articles in it devoted to the subject, implicating infection, sexual excess, chronic neuritis, and even the imagination of excitable young women.

The complete lack of progress in this condition was undoubtedly due to the difficulty of investigating the pelvis of women who were young and otherwise healthy. An operation inevitably involved removing an essentially normal organ, such as an ovary or the uterus, with a relatively small possibility of curing the pain.

A number of gynaecologists had come close to understanding the condition as a result of careful and methodical study, but even they were unable to do anything other than speculate that the likely cause of the condition was due to 'congestion' (like a bruise) in the pelvis. This was why they were unable to propose a suitable form of treatment, other than to say that surgery was rarely appropriate and should be avoided if possible.

Who Suffers?

Since establishing the Pelvic Pain Clinic at St Mary's Hospital, London, it has become apparent that a high proportion of our patients had experienced, or were experiencing, considerable emotional stress. A typical example is that of Mrs J, who came to us with chronic pain which she reported as having started after the birth of her daughter eleven years before. She was constantly aware of the pain, but occasionally it had been so bad that she had been admitted to hospital as an emergency. Although it had had a bad effect on all aspects of her life, the most damaging was the deterioration in the quality of her sex life – the pelvic pain which always started an hour after orgasm was unbearable so that she came to fear and eventually to avoid intercourse. Many gynaecologists had tried to help by prescribing antibiotics for possible pelvic infections or by performing exploratory operations at which nothing serious was found. Perhaps, she thought, it was time to consider a hysterectomy – not a pleasant prospect for a young woman of twenty-eight. Because of our interest in the stress factor in pelvic pain we discussed this possibility with Mrs J. and a typical story emerged. She had been a happy child, devoted to her father, until her parents divorced when she was eight. Her mother remarried and in her early teens she was molested by her step-father. At the age of fifteen she left home and by seventeen had been forced into marriage by pregnancy. For a time the marriage held together but the couple's extreme youth made adjustment difficult and they parted. After living alone with her daughter for some time she met a man with whom she had been for three years. This relationship was fundamentally happy but was threatened by her reluctance to have intercourse because of the pain that inevitably followed. She felt that they were drifting apart.

This story is not unique. Many women who come to the Pelvic Pain Clinic at St Mary's have even worse stories to tell. Others have had a normal happy childhood, and can date the pain from some deeply disturbing event, such as the loss of a close relative, or simply the arrival of a baby that had proved more than the woman could cope with. Whatever the origin, pelvic pain always seriously interferes with the life of the many young women who suffer from the condition.

Plan of Investigation

One of the first investigators in our group was a psychiatrist, who noted that women with pelvic pain, for which no obvious cause could be found, had a high level of neuroticism, strong dependent needs and a dislike of all matters sexual.

His early studies with relaxation therapy suggested that these women could learn to overcome their pain, either becoming completely pain-free, or being significantly improved. His work was continued by a psychologist, who carried out a number of treatment trials which clearly showed that at the end of a year of either relaxation or counselling seventy per cent of women showed significant improvement. Put quite simply, they had learnt to cope with stressful situations which seemed to bring on the pain.

The next breakthrough in our studies occurred with the development of pelvic venography. This technique involves the insertion of a long needle up the vagina, through the cervix and into the muscle of the uterus. Radio-opaque dye is injected and is rapidly carried away into the circulation. The injection of the dye can be seen by fluoroscopy on a television screen. In normal women, all the dye has virtually disappeared by the end of the injection. By contrast, we found that women with pelvic pain have greatly dilated pelvic veins, often up to five times the size of those in a normal woman, which retained dye for a significantly longer period.

This finding was so consistent, being present in more than eighty per cent of these women, that it was inevitable we should assume that dilated pelvic veins were likely to be the cause of the pain. The dull ache is very similar to the pain of which individuals with long-standing varicose veins in the legs complain. Surprisingly, or so it seemed at the time, women with dilated pelvic veins, more often than not, did not have varicose veins in the legs.

We became dissatisfied with pelvic venography, however, as a routine method of looking at the pelvic veins. Although it has the considerable advantage of allowing the patient to see the veins herself, (and often this is the first time that anything 'abnormal' has been found), it can be uncomfortable and for this reason we turned to ultrasound scanning.

Very soon it became apparent that dilated pelvic veins showed up well on the scans – so well that their diameter could be measured. The scan also showed a surprisingly new feature. More than half of these women had a ring of tiny 'cysts' encircling one or both ovaries. The appearances were very similar to those found in a condition known as the polycystic ovary syndrome (see p. 117).

This finding is not fully understood, particularly as the symptoms in the polycystic ovary syndrome are different from those in women suffering from pelvic pain; in addition, a third of the women we studied had apparently normal ovaries on ultrasound. Nevertheless, the association of the ovary in the condition of pelvic pain is not one of chance, and has allowed us to construct a hypothesis as to the cause of dilated pelvic veins.

The Hypothesis

Veins in the pelvis are peculiar in that they do not have the constrictive fibrous sheaths that veins elsewhere in the body have, nor do they have valves to stop the backflow of blood. This can be explained by the need for these veins to dilate, or enlarge, enormously during pregnancy, to meet the increased blood flow requirements of the developing uterus and baby.

Why pain from these enlarged veins is not a dominant feature in pregnancy, yet is in the non-pregnant woman, is explained by the difference in the rate at which the blood flows to the pelvis in the two states. In the non-pregnant woman, a much smaller volume of blood moves more slowly, which is likely to lead to oxygen deficiency, which may, in turn, give rise to pain.

The dilation of these veins probably occurs in response to the rapid rise of pregnancy hormones, such as oestrogen and progesterone, and it seems likely that, in women with pelvic pain, there is a chronic state of increased secretion of hormones by the ovaries, with resulting dilation of the veins.

The evidence that the hormone in question is likely to be oestrogen is quite strong. To prove that it is oestrogen, however, it is necessary to demonstrate that suppression of oestrogen results in the return of the pelvic veins to normal.

We are working at the moment on this using a hormone which is known to suppress temporarily ovarian function. We regard the loss of menstruation at the expected time as evidence that the ovarian function has been suppressed. To date we have treated twenty cases of pelvic pain and dilated pelvic veins of whom seventeen have stopped their periods, and sixteen have coincidentally lost their pain. We have done repeat pelvic venography in a few and, to date, all show narrowing of the veins and marked improvement in pelvic blood flow.

Evidence that it is the dilation of the veins which, in the end, is the cause of the pain is provided by the injection of a drug called dihydroergotamine into women having an acute attack of pelvic pain. The drug has been shown to cause narrowing of the veins with an improvement in blood flow. In all cases to date, administration has resulted in a dramatic temporary improvement in the pain.

An extension of our hypothesis is that there is a direct link between the emotional disturbance from which women with pelvic pain suffer and the dilation of the veins.

The function of the ovaries is controlled by a small gland at the base of the brain called the pituitary. This gland, in turn, is under the influence of the hypothalamus, which is the major control centre in the brain. The hypothalamus has many connections to other parts of the brain and it may be that signals are sent along this pathway which cause the ovaries to form cysts and secrete excess oestrogen. We have little evidence at present to support this concept, but it holds out exciting possibilities for providing scientific evidence to explain the mechanisms underlying 'stress-related' disorders.

Treatment

Many methods have been used to treat pelvic pain in the past, but the results have always been disappointing because the treatment was not based on an adequate understanding of the cause of the condition.

Pain has two important components which determine how it is interpreted by the sufferer. First, there is the stimulus, and obviously the more severe the stimulus, the more the patient will feel. The second, which is probably the most important when assessing the effect of a chronic low intensity pain, is the emotional state of the sufferer. The woman who is tense and anxious will inevitably complain of a severe pain even though the stimulus is relatively mild. Likewise, the well-adjusted 'prepared' woman will suffer severe pain without complaint.

This concept of the factors underlying pain response explains why we consider that some form of psychotherapy is an essential part of treatment for pelvic pain. In addition, if our hypothesis on the influence of the emotional state of the woman on reproductive hormone (gonadotrophin) secretion of the pituitary is correct, there is a further reason to use psychotherapy: to help these women to cope with environmental stress. However, it would be wrong to say we have found the final solution to the problem of pelvic pain. To date, two methods of treatment have been assessed.

Psychotherapy
The object of this is to produce a significant improvement in pain after no more than four visits. Two trials of a variety of forms of

psychotherapy have been undertaken. These trials have shown that simply reassuring a woman with pelvic pain after laparoscopy, that no cause can be found for her pain, results in only temporary improvement and that after three months the pain has usually returned in full force. The forms of psychotherapy that have proved to be effective up to a year later are relaxation, non-directive counselling, stress and pain analysis.

How psychotherapy acts is not known. It may be that the confidence of knowing that when pain appears it can be coped with and that it is not due to a life-threatening condition reduces the level of anxiety, and pain perception is, accordingly, diminished. Alternatively, as explained earlier, it may act by a more direct hormonal response, via the cortex of the brain and the pituitary, to regularize the function of the ovaries, eventually improving the pelvic blood flow.

Drugs
A drug called Provera (medroxyprogesterone acetate) is taken continuously over a six-month period to suppress the activity of both ovaries (based on the evidence already cited that too much oestrogen is secreted from the ovary). The great advantage of this drug is that it does not totally suppress ovarian activity, so there is always enough oestrogen in the circulation to prevent unpleasant side effects, such as flushes and sweating. The disadvantage is that in about fifteen per cent of women, this prevents ovarian activity being adequately suppressed. In practice, we have found that by using a dose of 30mg of Provera a day, complete suppression of menstruation was achieved in seventeen out of twenty women. Sixteen of these women became pain-free within eight weeks, while one, who was obese and therefore thought to be making oestrogen from her past stores, noted some improvement but did not become pain-free. The remaining three continued to have breakthrough bleeding, and continued to have pelvic pain.

These preliminary results have encouraged us to set up a prospective trial of treatment. We still do not know what the long-term results of such treatment will be, but we have some preliminary evidence to show that, while there is an improvement in the pelvic congestion, the pain may return after some time when treatment is stopped. This would suggest that a combination of ovarian suppression for a limited period of time, complemented by psychotherapy, has a good possibility of providing a lasting cure. More work is needed to determine the best form of treatment.

Chronic pelvic pain related to dilated pelvic veins is a common condition in women of reproductive age. It is characterized by emotional disturbance and several pelvic symptoms, which suggest that there is an underlying condition of vascular congestion.

Treatment with both psychotherapy and Provera, which suppresses ovarian function, has been found to relieve pain in more than seventy per cent of sufferers.

The condition seems likely to be an example of a 'stress-related disease', and may well explain not only a wide variety of gynaecological symptoms, but also some of the more perplexing cases referred by GPs to urologists or gastroenterologists.

More work is needed to characterize the condition in order to investigate fully the link between psyche and soma. If such a link can be demonstrated, the implications for a better understanding of many diseases affecting women are considerable.

21
Menstrual Disorders

Mary Ann Lumsden

'But nothing could easily be found that is more remarkable than the monthly flux of women. Contact with it turns new wine sour, crops touched by it become barren, the fruit of trees falls off, hives of bees die, even bronze and iron are at once seized by rust and the horrible smell fills the air; to taste it drives dogs mad, and infects their bites with an incurable poison.' (Attributable to Pliny, AD 20–80)

Menstrual problems are one of the most common causes of concern for women's health, a concern which is heightened by the many myths and taboos which surround the subject. Although the above quote is very ancient, taboos still exist today, exemplified by the exclusion of menstruating women from temples in parts of Malaysia and India. These problems have grown acute in this century: the reduction in family size has meant that women experience approximately ten times the number of periods than before, during the course of their reproductive life. With the changing role of women in society, it is not possible to be incapacitated on a regular basis, and once child-bearing is over, many women simply find their periods a nuisance.

A great many women suffer from disorders of menstruation and, although they are not often life-threatening, they can cause intense misery. Up until the last ten to fifteen years, however, treatment was limited to surgery, but recent research has led to the introduction of some very effective treatments, which mean that menstrual disorders need no longer be considered as a woman's lot in life.

What is a Normal Period?

A menstrual period is the regular shedding of the lining of the womb (endometrium) which occurs every twenty-one to thirty-five days and normally lasts between three and seven days. This process and other changes that occur during the cycle are controlled by hormones, or chemical messengers – two important ones being oestrogen and progesterone. These are produced by the ovary and are involved in the production of eggs as well as the preparation of the womb lining for implantation of the embryo if pregnancy occurs.

Generally there is no pregnancy, and it is the subsequent drop in these hormones which precedes the menstrual period. The tissue shedding is accompanied by bleeding from small blood vessels which are present in large numbers in the womb lining and the function of which is also dependent on the sex hormones. The amount of blood lost is controlled by constriction of these vessels. This in turn is affected by chemicals produced locally in the womb lining, as is discussed later. The bleeding is normally accompanied by contractions of the uterine (womb) muscles, which probably aid expulsion of the contents and can also be painful. Studies carried out on large groups of women who did not feel that they had any menstrual problems indicate that ninety-five per cent had a blood loss of under 80 ml per period; a loss over this amount was frequently associated with anaemia (when the blood becomes 'thin' and may be accompanied by tiredness and general debility). This level of blood loss is thus considered the upper limit of normal.

A 'normal' amount of pain is very difficult to define as pain tolerance varies between women and in the same woman on different occasions. The pain is due to overactivity of the womb muscle, as is described later. Some activity appears necessary during the period and it is difficult to say when this becomes too much. Most gynaecologists simply say, therefore, that if the pain leads to incapacity it is abnormal.

What causes Menstrual Problems?

Problems can occur at any time during the reproductive years. Heavy periods are particularly common around the time when periods first start and stop, i.e. at puberty and the menopause. This happens because the ovary is not working quite as efficiently as in the middle years and consequently the sex hormones are not produced in a regular fashion. Problems may also arise, however, because of some abnormality within the womb itself. These include fibroids (non-cancerous growths in the muscle wall), endometrial polyps (frond-like growths of the lining of the womb), infection and very rarely, malignancy (cancer).

Cancer of the endometrium occurs in about one woman in every 100,000 per year aged thirty-six or less, and is very rare in all women before the menopause. Any bleeding after the menopause should be reported to the doctor, but beforehand changes in the pattern or volume of menstrual loss are rarely sinister. The majority of cases of heavy periods (menorrhagia) are without an obvious physical cause and the reason why they occur relates to local substances produced by the endometrium and one group of these is known as prostaglandins. These can cause blood vessels to get bigger or smaller, thus affecting blood loss. An imbalance of these prostaglandins is now thought to be a major factor in heavy periods, particularly as their levels are affected by the reproductive hormones, notably oestrogen and progesterone. It is important to note that women with this imbalance have a womb which appears entirely normal and we do not know what causes the hormonal upsets. The levels of all the hormones circulating in the blood, including the sex hormones, appear normal except on the first day of the period when the amount of a hormone called vasopressin is increased. This hormone is very similar to oxytocin which is the hormone that makes the uterus contract in labour. As it causes increased activity of the womb muscle it may be involved in the induction of period pains.

Period pains (dysmenorrhoea) can also occur throughout reproductive life, although the cause tends to vary over the years; but it is more than just a pain: it is a complex of symptoms, the cramping, lower abdominal pain being frequently accompanied by backache, leg ache, stomach upsets and headaches. In young women, under twenty-five to thirty years, it tends once again to be due to an imbalance of prostaglandins. Apart from making the blood vessels smaller, these chemicals also make the womb muscle over-active and these properties together cause pain because not enough blood, with its oxygen and nutrients, can reach the muscle through the narrowed blood vessels.

In older women, however, a physical cause of period pains becomes much more likely. As with heavy periods, these include fibroids, polyps, infection or the presence of a foreign body, such as a contraceptive coil. In addition, there is a condition called endometriosis, which deserves special mention, as it is a relatively common cause of infertility and is easily treated (see p. 169). It tends to be more common in women in their thirties and occurs when little pieces of the womb lining start to grow elsewhere in the pelvis and abdomen. These bleed with each period, causing pain, and stick firmly to other organs nearby, causing physical distortion. Treatment involves giving special hormones which stop the bleeding and the tissue then shrivels up and dies. The other causes, apart from infection, are very rare in young women and it is a reasonable generalization to say that period pains in women under twenty-five are rarely associated with physical disease.

Consulting the Doctor

Every year thousands of women of all ages visit their own doctor or gynaecologist complaining of menstrual problems. Details will be taken of their menstrual cycles together with any recent changes in pattern. The doctor will ask about other gynaeco-logical problems – such as vaginal discharge, bleeding between periods or pain on intercourse – since these may help him or her work out the cause. For example, heavy, dark-coloured or odorous discharge may be associated with infection, or pain on intercourse with endometriosis. The doctor will also enquire about the number of previous pregnancies. Period pain without a physical cause is often relieved by the birth of a baby, and whether a person wishes further pregnancies or not will obviously influence treatment. A brief general history will then be taken to check for other problems which may be related to the cause or alter the treatment.

After the questions, a pelvic examination will be made. This will indicate the presence of physical abnormalities, but it is worth mentioning that in a plump or nervous patient it can be quite difficult. The doctor may order some simple tests. He may measure a substance in the blood called haemoglobin. This is low if you are suffering from anaemia, which in turn is associated with heavy periods. He may do some simple hormone tests to check how well the ovary is working. He may also organize admission to hospital for a dilatation and curettage (D & C), which is a simple procedure done under general anaesthetic, taking just a few minutes. It involves dilating the neck of the womb and scraping out the lining which can then be sent to the laboratory for tests.

Examination of the pelvis is also easier when the patient is anaesthetized (at D & C). However, D & C is of limited value in women under about thirty-five years. Cancer is very rare in this age group, as I have already stressed, and a D & C is not an effective treatment for heavy periods unless a polyp of the womb lining is present. There may be a reduction in menstrual loss initially, but the effect will wear off after a few months. In women of menopausal age, however, a D & C will be one of the early investigations. Under some circumstances, such as when endometriosis or infection is suspected, a laparoscopy will be performed at the same time. This involves putting some air into the abdomen and looking in with a special telescope. It usually means staying in hospital for about twenty-four hours, but this is well worthwhile as it gives a lot of useful information.

Treatment

Drugs
Frequently treatment is offered on the basis of the story and examination alone. Some drugs may be used for both heavy periods and period pains. As an imbalance of prostaglandins is implicated in both conditions, drugs which decrease their production would be an obvious possibility. These, known as non-steroidal-anti-inflammatory agents, are widely used and are very effective, particularly in dysmenorrhoea. Their advantages are that they need only be taken during the period, and side effects are thus reduced. These are usually mild and consist of nausea, indigestion and rashes. Serious side effects do occur when the drugs are taken on a continuous basis, as in the case of arthritis, but are virtually unheard of in those taking them for a few days each month.

The oral contraceptive pill also alters prostaglandin production and is often a useful treatment in the younger woman. The side effects are not discussed here, as most women are now aware of them.

Other drugs which may be offered include danazol, extensively used to treat endometriosis and also useful for menstrual disorders in general. It does produce numerous side effects, however, which although reversible, can be unpleasant. These include acne, fluid retention, weight gain, increased hair growth and skin rashes. In Scandinavia they are also trying drugs which block the action of the hormone vasopressin, although these drugs are not yet available here. Cyclical treatment with gestagen, which is just one of the hormones in the oral contraceptive pill, similar to progesterone, may be helpful in some cases. Also drugs are available which affect the clotting of blood (e.g. epsilon-amino-caproic acid and tranexamic acid) but these have annoying side effects such as nausea and vomiting and so are rarely used.

There are other drugs currently being tested which will be very important in the future. They are known as the luteinizing hormone-releasing hormone agonists (LHRH agonists) which switch off hormone production from the ovaries. They are useful in treating endometriosis and fibroids and give complete relief of menstrual problems. However, at the moment they can only be given for up to a year, and the problems seem to recur when they are stopped.

Surgery

The decision to perform a hysterectomy is one which is made jointly between gynaecologist and patient. Normally it is reached when the periods cause regular debility and are disrupting daily life.

The operation involves removing the womb with or without the ovaries and may be accomplished either by making a cut in the tummy (abdominal hysterectomy) or in the front passage (vaginal hysterectomy). The type of operation chosen depends on a number of factors. If the womb is enlarged (e.g. with fibroids), if there is another disease present (e.g. endometriosis or infection in the past), or if there have been previous operations (e.g. Caesarean section) then the route through the abdominal wall is usually chosen. If there are 'water works' problems with some prolapse, then the route through the front passage is preferable. Where none of these factors are present then the decision is the gynaecologist's. The recovery from vaginal hysterectomy is usually quicker than from the abdominal procedure, but if problems are encountered during the operation they are more difficult to sort out because the space is more restricted than when an incision has been made through the abdomen.

If the woman is under forty years of age at the time of the operation then, provided they are healthy, her ovaries are normally conserved. They will continue to produce the female hormones in a cyclical fashion as usual until about the time of the natural menopause. Over the age of forty then the decision of whether to remove the ovaries or not will usually be made after discussion between the gynaecologist and patient. If they are removed and menopausal symptoms occur then hormone replacement can be given with excellent results.

The number of deaths occurring as a result of hysterectomy for non-cancerous reasons is extremely small. Occasionally anaesthetists run into problems, or concurrent medical diseases get worse after the operation. Morbidity, however, is much more common. Usually it is minor with infections to the wound or 'water-works', although occasionally it can be more serious and lead to prolonged stays in hospital. These problems are unusual but should always be taken into consideration when making the decision to operate.

Pre-Menstrual Syndrome (PMS)

Very little is as yet known about the cause and successful treatment of pre-menstrual syndrome. PMS occurs when a patient has a symptom or group of symptoms before the period which is relieved when the period starts and during the early part of the cycle. The symptoms, which are not due to any physical abnormality, can be almost anything, although depression, fluid retention, soreness of the breasts and general malaise are probably the most usual. It appears to be a common condition, seriously incapacitating twenty to forty per cent of women, and possibly occurring to some extent in ninety per cent. Symptoms heralding a period were first noted by Hippocrates, and they are no respecter of persons since Queen Victoria herself may have been affected. As with other menstrual disorders, however, it is only in the last twenty years that doctors have started to take the problem seriously.

The cause is still unknown although most research has centred around an imbalance in the sex hormone levels. One of the most popular theories is a lack of progesterone in the week or two weeks before the period, when the symptoms are worse. PMS frequently starts after a major hormonal upset, such as pregnancy or stopping the oral contraceptive pill, and some cases can be effectively treated with hormones, as described later.

Consulting the Doctor
It is important for the doctor to know that the symptoms are due to PMS and not to some other disorder. This requires no complicated tests or investigations; you must simply keep a diary, and note when you suffered two or three major symptoms and when menstruation occurred. Charts can often be obtained from your GP for this purpose. A record must be kept for at least three months, because, unlike symptoms due to stress and life

events alone, PMS is a regularly recurring problem, and it is vital that the diagnosis is accurate for treatment to be effective.

Treatment
It was in the early 1950s that research indicated that PMS may be due to the presence of too little progesterone in the week or two weeks before the period. Many doctors therefore give either natural progesterone, or tablets containing progesterone-like drugs (progestagens), during this time. A major problem with this type of treatment, however, is that irregular bleeding can occur and can also make period pains worse.

Another avenue of research indicated that lack of Vitamin B6 (Pyridoxine) was important. This appeared so particularly when breast pain was a major symptom. Vitamin B6 can be taken in tablet form but should only be used as directed by the doctor as it can have serious side effects at high doses. The normal dose is 10 mg taken twice daily. Some women, however, feel that the more they take the better and take gram quantities of the vitamin which can be dangerous. Follow the dosage on the bottle. Recent research suggests that the oil of Evening Primrose may be very beneficial for PMS and side effects with this preparation are very few. In fact the placebo effect of little more than a doctor who is prepared to listen and take the problem seriously is enormous and gives positive relief in up to sixty per cent of sufferers.

Self-help may be an important part of the treatment too. Many sufferers comment that they tend to take their depression and irritability out on the immediate family. If the family understands the problem, it can be of real benefit. There are a number of organizations which produce leaflets especially for non-medical people, one or two of which are listed at the end of this book; it may be helpful if you were to get some and let the family read these too. Dietary manipulation, with small, frequent meals can help as some of the symptoms are similar to those which occur when the amount of sugar in the blood is low, including the craving for sweet things which many women experience. A large number of regions now have their own self-help groups to provide support and advice and you may find there is no need to visit your doctor at all.

The final type of treatment is symptomatic. For example, those with fluid retention can take special tablets which speed up water loss, and anti-depressants may be given to those with depression as a major symptom. The doctor may, however, be reluctant to prescribe these sort of tablets as PMS can be a very long-term problem.

Many hospitals now have special clinics dealing with PMS and other menstrual problems. Doctors in these clinics are likely to have access to the latest treatments and also have a particular interest in the subject, and if a sufferer is unhappy with the treatment she is receiving at present, it is well worth enquiring. Being told by the doctor to 'put up with it' should now be a thing of the past.

Fibroids

The medical name for fibroids is uterine leiomyomata. They are benign tumours of the womb muscle and are very common, occurring in up to twenty-five per cent of women of reproductive age. 'Benign tumour' essentially means a lump which is harmless, which is true to an extent, in that fibroids rarely become malignant (i.e. turn into cancer), but they are associated with a number of problems which I will describe below.

The first problem of fibroids is that they tend to get bigger. They may reach the size of a seven-month pregnancy, when they weigh about 4 lb (or 2 kg). They grow particularly during pregnancy because they are dependent on the presence of the hormone oestrogen and there is a lot of this about during pregnancy. Some fibroids cause problems and others don't, and the reason for this is unknown. The problems they are associated with are infertility, problems in pregnancy when it does occur, menstrual problems and non-specific problems. However, it is very important to realize that not all fibroids, whatever their shape, size or number, show symptoms. Some are noticed only when the woman is examined, for example, in the family planning or well woman clinic.

Fibroids may occur singly or in large numbers in the uterus. They distort the shape both of the muscle and the cavity within the womb. This may be the reason why they can cause relative infertility, although they are not a common cause of infertility unless associated with other problems. When pregnancy does occur, miscarriage is more common than in the normal population, and if they enlarge during pregnancy, as they tend to do, they may interfere with delivery. When they are known to be present, additional care can be taken during pregnancy and many of the problems can thus be avoided.

By far the most common problems associated with fibroids are menstrual. These may involve heavy periods, period pains or both together. Menstrual problems occur in about one third of those with fibroids and many of the standard drug treatments described in the 'Treatment' section tend to be ineffective. About the same proportion of women with fibroids complain of pelvic pain or pressure symptoms and, very rarely, there may be interference with bowel or bladder functions.

The reason why fibroids occur is unknown, which makes a cure difficult to find. Up until recently the only treatment has been surgery, either involving removal of the fibroids alone (myomectomy) in a woman wishing to maintain her fertility, or hysterectomy. However, a new medical treatment is now being tested. This is a drug called luteinizing hormone-releasing hormone agonist (LHRH agonist) which is a chemical synthesized in the laboratory and similar in structure to a hormone produced naturally in all women. When administered continuously it switches off production of oestrogen by the ovaries and since fibroid growth is dependent on the presence of oestrogen, they get smaller. The drug can be given by monthly injection and within six months, the fibroids either shrink dramatically or disappear. Unfortunately, since the drug effectively produces a temporary menopause, it can only be used for a few months as menopausal side effects occur. The most important of these is thinning of the bones, a common post-menopausal problem (see Chapter 23). This very much limits the use of the drug as the fibroids regrow after the treatment is stopped. We feel it may be useful in women wishing to avoid a hysterectomy, either because they are unfit for surgery or who are near the menopause, when fibroids are known to shrink naturally. In a recent study published in the Lancet we demonstrated that the use of LHRH agonist for three months prior to hysterectomy made the operation and immediate post operative period easier. Another approach is to use it in combination with other agents in order to minimize side effects, but this is very much in the experimental stage. The LHRH agonists are not a cure for fibroids, but they provide excellent relief from menstrual problems and considerable fibroid shrinkage while they are being used. We are also busy looking for the reason why they are there at all, but the answer to this, I think, is a long way off.

22
Hirsutism – Excessive Hair

Michael G. Chapman

The modern woman is extremely conscious of her appearance. Her skin is of major concern, and fashion dictates that facial and body hair is a significant blemish. A large number of women are affected to a greater or lesser degree, but because of embarrassment, few admit their problem to others. The majority hide it, often because they fear that a hormonal imbalance may be the underlying cause. The presence of unwanted hair, therefore, causes substantial emotional and psychological grief, and the feeling that it is abnormal is reinforced by magazines which inform women with excessive hair of the many cosmetic aids for its removal. Suggestions of hormonal imbalance as the underlying cause are common, so that many are led to believe that in some way they are becoming 'male', and an increasing number of women are seeking medical advice in the belief that there is a serious underlying problem. In fact, in all but the very severe cases it is extremely rare to find a significant hormone disease, although in many a slight imbalance can be demonstrated.

The Physiology of Hair Growth

Men and women are born with the same number of hair follicles in the skin, and how active they become depends on their reaction to the male hormone testosterone, which is present in both men and women. In the male as the teenage boy passes through puberty, testosterone levels increase dramatically with various noticeable effects, including voice change and increased musculature. Facial and body hair begins to appear when the hair follicle is exposed to these increasing levels of testosterone.

Testosterone levels also rise in the female during puberty, but to a far lesser extent than in the male: in most women it will simply stimulate the growth of pubic and underarm hair. About fifteen per cent of women, however, develop hair in areas outside the 'normal' pattern. In the vast majority this is a genetic predisposition, probably related to an inherited sensitivity of the hair follicle to normal levels of testosterone. A prime example is the racial differences seen in body hair: Scandinavian and Japanese women, for example, rarely have facial hair, but those from the southern Mediterranean countries and the Indian subcontinent will often have excess hair by our Western standards.

Once the follicle has been programmed to produce hair it will continue to respond to almost any level of male hormone which is present, even though this level may be in the normal range. The follicle has become committed to producing hair in the long term. This makes treatment difficult (see below).

Each hair follicle goes through phases of active growth and then of rest. On the face, this happens over a period of six to nine months with each hair filament. Only a small percentage of the follicles present in a particular area will be in the active stage at any one time, so that the overall hair grown represents only a small proportion of the potential hair in that area. This has implications when cosmetic measures are used to treat the hair.

To understand the processes of excessive hair growth, we must look in greater detail at how hormones control hair growth. In the female, male hormones are normally produced by the adrenal gland and the ovaries. Some are also formed from the conversion of other hormones in the fat tissues of the body. The most important male hormone is probably testosterone, although there are a series of other related compounds. Ninety-eight per cent of the testosterone in the blood is attached to proteins, predominantly sex hormone-binding globulin (SHBG), and as such is inactive. It is only the tiny unattached fraction which activates the hair follicle, and to do this the testosterone must link to the special sites (receptors) on the cells of the follicle. Once in the cell, the testosterone is converted to other stronger male hormones which act on the cell nucleus (or growth centre) to activate growth. Abnormalities in any of these various steps may contribute to excessive hair growth.

Seeking Help

If you are worried by increased hair growth you should consult your doctor. Many women are reluctant to do so because it is an embarrassing problem, even though it may be causing serious emotional upset. Women who think their hair is disfiguring may avoid social contact, stay indoors and become depressed. They may feel very alone. A major worry for some is that they are 'becoming male', and reassurance that they are not is a significant step in coming to terms with the problem. Your doctor should be able to provide such help, but unfortunately this is not always so. Many doctors have not been educated about this particular problem and do not realize the anguish it can produce. If you do not receive satisfaction, tell the doctor that you are still worried and would like a further opinion. He or she may refer you to a dermatologist, a gynaecologist or an endocrinologist.

What will the doctor ask?
Naturally the specialist will want to know about the extent of the growth, i.e. face, abdomen, breasts. The length of time it has been present is important. If it has been there since your teens it is unlikely that there will be a serious hormonal problem. He or she will ask about the treatments you have used. Some women find this embarrassing and are reluctant to say. They often feel that shaving is 'unnatural' and incorrectly imagine that they may even be making the problem worse. It is important for the doctor to know, however, because it helps in his or her assessment of the problem.

The regularity of periods is another significant feature. If the cycle is regular, it is extremely unlikely that there is any serious hormonal abnormality. A family history of similar problems will be important. If your mother or aunts have hirsutism it is likely that the problem is hereditary, although this does not mean that they will be the same – genetic predisposition is handed on in a variable manner – but, however serious, help can usually be provided. Racial background is another likely cause; one of the problems in our multiracial society is that women with normal hair distribution for their race feel abnormal because of the Western perception of 'normal'.

The doctor may also enquire about drugs that you have taken. Certain tablets cause increased hair growth in some women. For instance, danazol, which is used in the treatment of endometriosis (see p. 169) will induce mild hirsutism in about ten per cent of patients. Your doctor will be able to find out whether tablets that you have been taking for any length of time might be a factor in the hair growth.

Will the doctor want to examine me?
Yes, and although you may find it embarrassing, it is necessary for him or her to do so in order to assess properly the extent of your problem. Vaginal examination may also be helpful to the doctor since some cases of severe hirsutism are related to abnormalities of the ovary which may be enlarged.

Will the doctor check my hormone levels?
This will vary depending upon the doctor and on the severity of your hair growth. In my own practice I would at least carry out one blood test to check the level of male hormone. For ninety-nine per cent of women with hirsutism the result will be reassuring, the level being in the normal female range or just above. It certainly will be well below the normal male range.

At the end of all these questions, examinations and tests, it is almost certain that the worst that will be found will be a mild hormone imbalance.

Treatment

From the cosmetic viewpoint much can be done to improve the situation. To the outside world, at least, the impact of excessive hair can be diminished considerably.

Bleaches
By lightening the hair colour, the growth becomes less obvious. Fair-haired women with hirsutism have much less of a problem than darker-haired women. Many bleaches are available at the local chemist, but take care when using one on the face. The skin is sensitive and can react to some chemicals, so test it first on an unexposed area.

Waxes
Removal of hair by waxing is well recognized, and a number of products are on the market, primarily for use on the arms, legs and body. They tend to be painful, however, and application to the face is difficult; once again skin sensitivity can be a problem.

Plucking
This is the most common method of control on the face. Unfortunately, it is very time-consuming and can be painful.

Shaving
Although many women regard shaving as masculine and therefore unacceptable, it can certainly keep the hair at bay in more
serious cases. Despite 'old wives' tales' to the contrary, scientific
studies have shown that shaving does not increase the rate of hair
growth or the thickness of the hair. These tales arise from the fact
that the base of the hair filament tends to be thicker so that when
hair first grows back, having been shaved, it appears to be
thicker.

Electrolysis
This is the most effective cosmetic method of reducing hair
growth. A small electric current is sent down each hair filament in
turn and the hair follicle in the skin is destroyed. Since only a tiny
percentage of the hair follicles are active at any one time,
however, only a small number are destroyed at each treatment
session. In addition, the burning can cause a tiny spot of redness
in the skin together with a little discomfort. Treatments, therefore, tend to be of only ten to fifteen minutes' duration, which
means that to rid an area of follicles takes a long time. It is
important to go to a qualified therapist for electrolysis, since
excessive burning can cause pain and scarring. In the UK
treatment is sometimes available on the National Health Service,
but mostly it is carried out privately in beauty salons, which can
obviously be expensive over the long period required to produce
good results.

Treatment with drugs
An alternative approach is to use drugs – usually hormones. You
will recall from the section on the physiology of hair growth that
there are a series of steps in the stimulation of the hair follicle. By
altering some of these processes with drugs, it is possible in some
cases to slow down or even halt the hair growth. For instance, by
taking certain oral contraceptive pills the liver is stimulated to
make more binding protein, and this will 'mop up' any male
hormone in the circulation, and for some women this treatment is
sufficient to improve the hirsutism.
    A further approach is to inhibit the action of the male hormone
when it reaches the hair follicle. There are two drugs currently
used in this manner – cyproterone acetate and Spironolactone.
These both require relatively high doses and should only be used
under the direction of an expert in such hormone therapy. In
eighty per cent of cases, an improvement in hair can be expected.
These drugs do have side effects and, although they are not

dangerous, tiredness and depression are not uncommon. Close liaison with your doctor is necessary.

Another treatment that has been tried with some success is the use of steroids.

All these drugs, however, will maintain improvement while the tablets are being taken, but when they are stopped it is common for the problem to recur to a greater or lesser extent. This is because the drugs do not have a long-term effect on the sensitivity of the hair follicle to male hormones in the circulation. They only work while the drugs are in the circulation. Nevertheless, the problem does not always recur and this method can correct the hormone imbalance and provide a long-term cure.

Length of treatment

The length of time on treatment is determined by the response of the hair and to some extent by your own feelings about taking hormones. Generally a change in the hair character is only noted after six to nine months of treatment. This slow response is due to the fact that the drugs only affect newly growing hair, and as explained earlier, new hair takes this sort of time scale to develop. After reduction in hair growth, most doctors would continue treatment for a further twelve to eighteen months. A rest is often suggested at that point to assess whether the improvement is to be sustained. If a recurrence occurs, treatment can be started again.

The first sign that treatment is working successfully is when the time between cosmetic treatments becomes longer. Whereas bleaching may have been necessary every other day, for example, you will find you need to do it only once a week. The hair filaments begin to lighten and become thinner. They are not so tough to remove and their return is slower. As stated before, the degree of improvement is variable. Sometimes whole patches of hair may disappear; in other cases, the improvement may only be related to the change in texture and colour.

For most women there is an improvement in hirsutism during pregnancy due to the high oestrogen levels that are present. This benefit sometimes persists after childbirth.

If you are worried you should seek help, although many GPs know little about hirsutism. If you are not satisfied with his or her response, ask to be referred to a specialist centre. It is rare for a serious hormonal cause to be present, and for the vast majority cosmetic and drug treatment can improve the situation.

23
Menopause and Osteoporosis

John W. W. Studd

The years around the menopause are a period of tranquillity for
many women, but a time of torment for the majority. Robert
Browning's exhortation 'Grow old along with me, the best is yet
to be', takes a somewhat poetic view of old age as many serious
causes of ill health occur in the wake of the menopause.
Fortunately, although it is frequently a time of great problems,
the challenging fact is that they are nearly all preventable and the
concept of oestrogen replacement for post-menopausal women is
one of the most exciting aspects of preventative medicine this
century.

The menopause refers to the time when the periods cease and
occurs on average at the age of fifty-one. It is accompanied by
many physical and psychological symptoms associated with lack
of oestrogen and several long-term metabolic defects, of which
osteoporosis (brittle bones) is the most important. Occasionally
the menopause may occur many years before this average age
and a premature menopause at the age of twenty-five is not a
rarity. Women with this early failure of the ovaries obviously
suffer from infertility and symptoms which are not only more
prolonged but also, because of the unusual age, are frequently
undiagnosed, and the appropriate treatment is not given.

Changes in the Body Tissues

When the ovaries fail, blood oestrogen levels fall and all the
tissues in the body dependent on adequate levels of female
hormones atrophy (begin to waste). In the pelvis the tissue of the
vulva and the vagina thin, producing the characteristic

symptoms of vaginal dryness during intercourse and painful intercourse. Similarly, the tissues of the bladder become thin and irritable, hence the problems of urinary frequency, pain on passing water with urgency and leakage on coughing. These are all problems which can be easily treated with replacement oestrogen (see p. 184).

Circulatory Symptoms

Apart from the local atrophic changes, the well-known problems of hot flushes and night sweats characterise the years around the menopause. We do not know the exact cause of these most distressing symptoms, which are not only a great embarrassment but also produce insomnia, with the woman waking up several times a night and starting the morning exhausted. These changes also, by their effect on brain vessels, produce the headaches and migraine which are common after the menopause. The circulation into the limb extremities is also reduced, except when the woman experiences a sudden loss of control or flush, which causes a temporary increase in blood flow and rapid increase in skin temperature. Mysterious though they are, there is no doubt that these problems can also be effectively treated with small doses of oestrogen.

Psychological Problems

The extent of the psychological symptoms of the menopause are perhaps more controversial. The age of fifty is often a difficult time for men and women facing problems of work, children and parents and frequently taking an increasingly pessimistic view of their own body image. It is thus often a time of considerable insecurity, which is made immeasurably worse by the coexisting hormonal changes of the menopause. There is an excess of depression manifested by the fact that half the women of this age group are taking tranquillizers and antidepressants. This is tragic because the considerable psychological problems of this age are frequently the result of the hormonal changes and the brutalizing symptoms of depression – loss of energy, loss of confidence, irritability and loss of libido – can and should be corrected with oestrogens rather than with psychoactive drugs, which have appalling side effects and problems of addiction.

Skin and Bone

After the menopause women lose collagen (a sticky protein which effectively keeps the cells of the body together) at the rate of one to three per cent per year. This is most obvious in its effect upon the skin, which becomes thin and wrinkled, with the translucent appearance of the elderly. Women of this age also frequently complain that their nails are brittle and their hair falls out. This observation is very common and very important because of the link between loss of collagen, as seen in the skin, nails and hair, and post-menopausal osteoporosis.

Some of the exciting information that has recently been obtained demonstrates that not only does long-term therapy prevent loss of collagen but also, even if started many years after the menopause, oestrogen therapy can put back all of the collagen lost from the skin within nine months. This has more than just cosmetic implications: the skin will be more healthy, it will heal better and there will be no more hair loss. Whether oestrogen therapy prevents the loss of collagen from other tissues in the body apart from the skin remains to be seen, but it is logical that it should.

The major long-term consequence of the menopause is that this loss of collagen and calcium from the bones leads to increased numbers of fractures which occur, even with minor stress. The bones particularly susceptible to this problem are the hip, the wrist and the spine. Twenty-five per cent of women aged sixty, and fifty per cent of women aged seventy, will have suffered one or more osteoporotic fractures.

Osteoporosis is a disorder peculiar to women. The ovaries fail earlier and more dramatically than the testes in men, which fail gradually at a later age, with the result that women suffer fractured hips and spines almost twenty times more frequently than men. At the age of seventy, women have lost fifty per cent of the mineral from their skeleton, but even at the age of ninety men have only lost twenty-five per cent. The thinning of the vertebrae produces painful crush fractures and loss of height and curvature of the spine (the so-called Dowager's Hump).

The magnitude of the problem can be appreciated if we confine ourselves to fracture of the hip, an injury which occurs in twenty-five per cent of women aged seventy and which causes considerable pain, disability and morbidity. Following a fractured hip thirty per cent of women die in the year after the injury, and in those who survive forty per cent do not walk again or have severe limitation of their mobility. To put this into perspective, more women die of fractured hips than die of cancer of the breast, ovary and cervix combined. The extraordinary fact about this condition is that the cause is known, and the means of preventing it is known, and in spite of this fifteen thousand women in the United Kingdom will have a fractured hip each year. Apart from the pain, suffering and death, this problem costs the nation £180 million per year – more than enough to run six large district general hospitals.

The Heart

Before the menopause women have a virtual immunity to heart attacks unless they smoke or have abnormal lipid (or fat) patterns. Following the menopause the lipid levels become abnormal and the frequency of heart attacks approaches that of men. It is hoped that oestrogen therapy will prevent this. We know that oestrogen replacement clearly modifies the cholesterol and lipid patterns in the post-menopausal woman in a beneficial way, and there are now some long-term studies emerging from epidemiologists at Oxford to indicate that deaths from heart attacks and also strokes are indeed less in women having hormone replacement therapy. Such good news requires confirmation by other very large detailed studies, but if confirmed it would give, together with the osteoporosis story, a very convincing argument for prolonged oestrogen therapy in the majority of post-menopausal women.

Oestrogen Treatment

The treatment for the problems of the menopause is essentially oestrogen replacement, but there are other serious considerations. It is important that women maintain healthy lifestyles with exercise, without smoking, without excess alcohol intake and keep up interests outside work and the home.

Before prescribing oestrogens it is important for the doctor to give the appropriate advice about general health care and to ensure that there are no serious contra-indications, such as hormone dependent cancers of the breast or lining of the womb. There are not many conditions that prevent the use of oestrogens. Other medical problems, such as hypertension, diabetes, previous thrombosis or obesity, are not a contra-indication provided natural oestrogens are used. There is no evidence that these hormones cause deterioration in these conditions. The woman should also have a general check-up of breasts, pelvis, cervical smear, blood pressure and urine, which really is no more than any woman should ideally have on a regular annual basis. There is usually no need for hormone tests before starting therapy and no need for any preliminary biopsy of the lining of the womb either. These are unnecessary and are effectively an obstacle between the patient and the simple straightforward treatment that she requires.

Oestrogens may be given by tablets, in a cream, by skin patches or by implants. All are effective. The different methods may be chosen for convenience, availability and for the blood levels of the various oestrogens that each one produces. All oestrogens used should be natural – those which occur naturally in the body – such as oestrone, oestradiol or oestriol. Synthetic oestrogens, like those found in the birth control pill, are much cheaper, but they are inappropriate and should not be used on older women. Unlike the natural oestrogens, they have unwanted effects upon clotting, cholesterol and glucose tolerance, and the older the woman is the more she is at risk from these complications.

Women who have had a total hysterectomy take oestrogen tablets every day. Continuous therapy for women who still have a uterus, however, will cause overstimulation of the lining of the womb (endometrium) and irregular troublesome bleeding. The anxiety at one time that oestrogens were a cause of uterine cancer was because they were being given alone without the cyclical opposition from progestogens. It is thus necessary to add progestogen tablets for seven to thirteen days each month to stop this overstimulation. This means that there will be a regular withdrawal bleed which is unlikely to bother women, as long as the bleed is not excessive and not painful. It is clear now that cancer of the uterus is less common in women having both oestrogens and progestogens than the overall population.

Oestrogen tablets certainly have the advantage of convenience and most women attending their GPs will be given this sort of therapy. Treatment by hormone implant inserted under local anaesthesia through the skin, however, is now becoming increasingly popular. It is a simple technique, painless and has to be repeated every six months. The metabolic effects are better because in bypassing the gut and the liver, there are no unwanted modifications to the hormone levels. Some patients experience nausea with the tablets and find an oestradiol implant far more acceptable.

If testosterone, a male hormone, is to be given it must be done as an implant, as testosterone by mouth is probably unsafe. This would be particularly appropriate for women who have had an inadequate response to oestrogen tablets or who complain of loss of energy, loss of libido, depression or headaches. Despite the considerable advantages of this method of administration, however, hormone implantation is not going to be available to the majority of women because of financial considerations. The alternative which has been devised is a hormone patch, which is kept on the skin for three days and then replaced. So far the results look very promising.

For how long?

The benefits of oestrogen therapy will be maintained for as long as the woman takes oestrogens. When she stops her symptoms and the unwanted metabolic and bone effects begin again, but if she has taken oestrogen for only five years, at least she has delayed the onset of osteoporosis by those five years. It does seem very logical to continue oestrogen therapy for twenty years or so. In reality, it is the woman who decides when to stop. If she is content with taking oestrogens by tablets, patch or implant over the years and is deriving symptomatic benefit from the medication without side effects, she should continue. On the other hand, if she feels no better or has side effects, such as irregular bleeding, she might well want to discontinue the treatment.

24

Urinary Incontinence

Stuart L. Stanton

Urinary incontinence is an embarrassing condition. It is also surprisingly common – about five to ten per cent of all women suffer – but although it interferes with lifestyle and independence, it is not life-threatening.

In many cases it is readily curable, but because some patients regard incontinence as a social stigma, and many doctors and nurses still fail to give it sufficient emphasis or importance when consulted, patients often hesitate for years before seeking advice.

The problem can start in a number of ways. It can be a 'teenager' who discovers that exercise makes her incontinent, or the younger woman who becomes incontinent after her first or second delivery. It is aggravated by the menopause, and sometimes may occur for the first time in later life. Whatever the cause, its incidence and severity increase with advancing years: a reason, perhaps, for seeking early medical advice.

It used to be thought that physical effort was the main trigger for urinary incontinence. Nowadays we appreciate that it is not so straightforward, and the diagnoses have become more numerous and complicated.

Basically the female anatomy is to blame. The mechanism of urinary control is unfortunately not very efficient in the female, and is not always sufficient to withstand the strains and stresses of exercise, even before pregnancy and labour.

Urine is formed in the kidneys and conveyed by two tubes (ureters), to the bladder, which is a muscular and contractile organ (not unlike a balloon). Urine is stored there until it is socially convenient to empty it. A muscular tube (urethra) leads from the bladder, and at the junction of the two (bladder neck) there is a muscular sphincter (urinary sphincter) which keeps urine in the bladder.

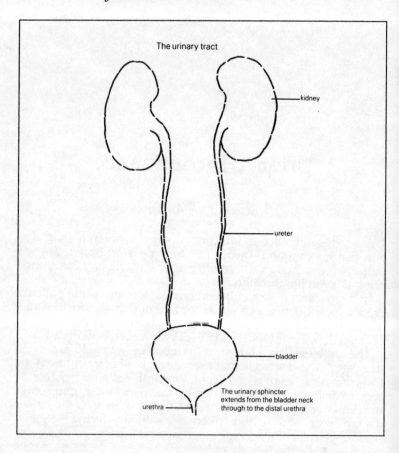

The urinary tract

kidney

ureter

bladder

The urinary sphincter
extends from the bladder neck
through to the distal urethra

urethra

Causes

Incontinence can happen for a number of reasons. It can be failure of the urethra to remain closed (urethral sphincter incompetence); it can be because the bladder contracts abnormally and forces urine past the closed sphincter (bladder instability); or a combination of both conditions.

Other less common causes include temporary incontinence associated with infection of the bladder (cystitis), which can be cleared up with appropriate drugs; and, more rarely, incontinence may be caused by an abnormal connection between the bladder and vagina (a fistula), resulting from surgery or disease in the pelvis.

Urethral sphincter incompetence

This is where the sphincter muscles fail to close the bladder neck at times of physical effort or stress, e.g. jogging, coughing or carrying a heavy load. It can happen spontaneously, or following childbirth when the neck of the bladder has descended abnormally low in the pelvis. It is often aggravated at the menopause by a decrease in production of the female hormone oestrogen, which normally nourishes the lining of the urethra and enhances the strength of muscles and ligaments supporting the bladder neck.

The most common symptom is stress incontinence (losing urine on exertion). There may be urgency (sudden desire to pass urine) and frequency (need to pass urine more frequently during the day or night); or there may be descent of the bladder, uterus or rectum, which can also begin after childbirth and is called prolapse. Any of these may produce a sensation of dragging in the vagina.

Bladder instability

The cause of this is uncertain. It may be due to a disorder of the nerve supply to the bladder, or it may be brought on by anxiety or mental stress. In some patients, the cause may be unknown. Therefore treatment and prognosis may vary.

The bladder, instead of acting as a container to store urine, may suddenly and involuntarily contract and force urine past the urinary sphincter. The main complaint is a sudden desire to empty the bladder which, if not fulfilled immediately, leads to un-controlled bladder emptying (urge incontinence). This is partic-ularly distressing, as the patient has little time, if any, to act. The urge may be triggered off by seeing water running (during washing-up, for example) or by putting the key into the front door.

The other complaints, which may coexist, are frequency and stress incontinence. If incompetence of the urethral sphincter and bladder instability are present together, the patient will have a mixture of these symptoms and correct diagnosis can only be made with the help of specialized investigations.

Infection

The female bladder is more susceptible to urinary infection than the male. The principal complaints are pain while passing urine (dysuria), frequency and urgency. In some women, the fre-quency and urgency may be so severe that urinary leakage occurs before toilet facilities are reached. It tends to be more common in the older woman, and is reversed by appropriate antibiotic or drug therapy.

Fistula

Occasionally as a result of surgery or disease in the pelvis, an abnormal channel may form between the vagina and urethra, bladder or ureter. This causes continuous incontinence, but the history is not always straightforward, and there may be co-incidental complaints of stress incontinence and urgency. It is a condition which needs careful investigation before any treatment can be given.

Treatment

In general, treatment will depend upon the causes of the incontinence. It is reasonable to say, however, that nowadays no patient should have to endure incontinence or have treatment refused because of her age, although clearly the patient must be sufficiently alert to appreciate the need to be dry.

There are a variety of treatments: general treatments include provision of pads, pants and catheter drainage; and specific treatment includes pelvic floor exercises, surgery, drug therapy, bladder retraining and biofeedback.

General treatment

Pads and pants have undergone a minor revolution since the bulky, ineffective and conspicuous designs of the past. They are now well-made and tailored, available in many different designs, according to the severity of the incontinence, the size of the patient and her personal preference. Crude wadding has given way to pads made of absorbent gel, which will contain many times their volume of water.

Pants are made of fine, washable elastic mesh, in a variety of designs and sizes. Alternatively, there are stout waterproof pants with pouches for large incontinence pads. Pads are ideal where either incontinence is minimal or where other forms of treatment have failed or are inappropriate.

Where incontinence is continuous and resistant to conventional treatment, a catheter (drainage tube) will provide certain and simple relief. New catheters are made of Silastic, an inert material, which resists the formation of debris inside the catheter and it may not need to be changed for up to four to six weeks. Usually the catheter is inserted into the urethra, but some women find it uncomfortable to wear, and some complain that it impedes sexual intercourse. As an alternative, it can be inserted through a small incision in the abdominal wall (suprapubic catheter).

Either way, the catheter is usually attached by tubing to a leg bag, and again various designs and sizes are available: a larger bag for use at night, and a smaller size for day wear.

Specific treatment

Incompetence of the urinary sphincter can be managed by one or all of the following: pelvic floor exercises, oestrogen replacement in the post-menopausal woman, and surgery.

PELVIC FLOOR EXERCISES

This requires considerable self-motivation and daily practice for at least three months if you hope to get anywhere. There are many forms of exercise. I prefer to teach the patient to feel her urinary sphincter work by asking her to interrupt her urinary stream during normal bladder emptying. Some women find this easy; others more difficult. Having mastered the exercise, she should then practise contracting the pelvic floor like this at other times during the day, until she is doing the exercise three to four times a day, for at least fifteen minutes each time.

This is most likely to help the younger woman. It is strenuous, but not more than any athlete would attempt when he or she wished to improve muscle strength in any other part of the body.

TAMPON

Women who have stress incontinence at moments of sudden exercise and strain may be able to prevent it by inserting a tampon into the vagina before taking exercise. This will have the effect of elevating the neck of the bladder, which is the main aim of surgery in these cases (see below).

OESTROGEN REPLACEMENT

For the older woman, a three-month trial of oestrogen replacement may alleviate mild stress and urge incontinence. It is important to ensure, however, that there is no contra-indication to this treatment; and if your uterus is still present, be prepared for a monthly withdrawal 'period' which will last a few days at the end of the course.

SURGERY

Surgery remains the main treatment for incompetence of the urinary sphincter, with a cure rate of up to ninety-five per cent in the young to middle-aged patient, who has never had previous surgery, and about eighty per cent for the patient who has.

The aim is to elevate the neck of the bladder to a higher position

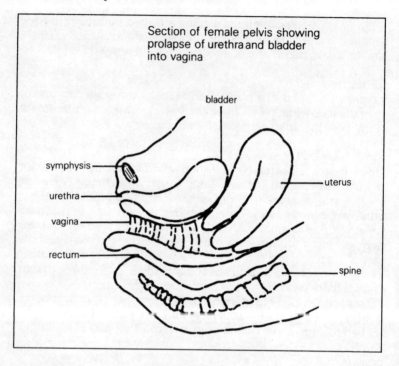

Section of female pelvis showing prolapse of urethra and bladder into vagina

bladder

symphysis

urethra

vagina

rectum

uterus

spine

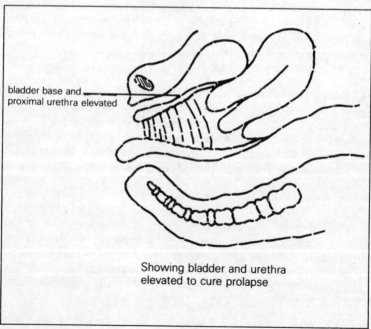

bladder base and proximal urethra elevated

Showing bladder and urethra elevated to cure prolapse

in the pelvis. This may correct any associated bladder prolapse as well. There is controversy here because traditionally gynaeco-logists have sought to do this by a vaginal repair operation. Current medical opinion, however, suggests that for many patients, an improved and more permanent cure may result from surgery carried out through the abdominal wall (suprapubic approach). My preference is for this route. There are many techniques, each surgeon having his own preference and having developed a particular expertise.

In general, if childbearing is incomplete, it is wiser to defer surgery and opt for pelvic floor exercises as an interim measure. This is because further deliveries may disrupt the repair, and subsequent surgery has a lower success rate. If you don't want to defer surgery, it would be advisable to have a Caesarean section for any subsequent delivery.

You will normally be required to stay in hospital for seven to ten days after the operation, but it depends ultimately on how soon normal bladder emptying returns. Most surgeons insert a urinary catheter after the operation, either via the urethra, or the abdominal wall (as described above). I prefer the latter, as I find patients regain bladder control earlier that way and with less risk of infection.

If possible, you are advised to convalesce for six to eight weeks after the operation with no heavy lifting during that period at all, so that the tissues have a chance to unite firmly in their new position. Some operations make intercourse uncomfortable (dyspareunia) for a while afterwards, so it is wiser to avoid it altogether for about the same length of time.

DRUG THERAPY
The best way to treat bladder instability if it is caused by a disorder of the bladder's nerve supply is with drugs. Those commonly prescribed are anti-spasmodic (e.g. Propantheline and Oxybutynin hydrochloride) and act on several organs, sometimes producing side effects such as a dry mouth, blurred vision and constipation.

To be effective, these drugs often have to be taken at their maximum level; and their success rate is variable. It depends on the individual patient, the dosage being given, and the strength of the bladder contractions. About fifty to sixty per cent of patients will show an improvement.

BLADDER RETRAINING
This works on the principle that the bladder has acquired an

altered rhythm and habit, and is responding prematurely to
bladder filling by signalling to the brain that it is full, when it
really is not.

Initially the patient is asked to complete a bladder chart for a
week, showing on a daily basis, how much fluid is taken, how
much urine is passed, and in what amount; also how often
episodes of urgency and urge incontinence occur.

From this chart the doctors and nurses will suggest a routine of
regular bladder emptying at increasing intervals, eventually
aiming for a two-to-three-hour gap. At the same time, the patient
has to attempt to inhibit her bladder urgency. Often she will be
admitted to hospital for a week, so that she can have the intensive
care and support of the medical and nursing staff while this re-
education takes place. The success rate is over eighty per cent.

BIOFEEDBACK

This is a method of treatment initially taught in hospital and used
to control many of the body's activities. In the case of retraining
the bladder, the patient has to see and hear signals from the
bladder when it is producing abnormal contractions – and she is
taught how to inhibit those contractions.

It involves being catheterised for an hour every week for about
eight weeks, which is not always acceptable to the patient, but
the success rate of this method of retraining is in excess of eighty
per cent.

Availability of Treatment

The medical profession has realized the importance of managing
incontinence correctly in recent years, and many health districts
now have specially trained nurses called 'continence nurse
advisers' on their staff. These nurses often work in close
collaboration with gynaecologists and urologists at the district
hospital. Your GP should know if there is one in your district.

Alternatively, he or she may advise you to consult a gynaecologist or urologist, who has a special interest in incontinence at
your local hospital, or at another hospital which has a specialized
centre for these conditions.

The expectation of cure is better than it was ten years ago, but
the need to improve further is a constant stimulus to research in
this area.

Birthright:
Useful Names and Addresses

National Association for Pre-menstrual Syndrome,
25 Market Street,
Guildford,
Surrey.

Women's Health Information Centre,
52 Featherstone Street,
London EC1.

Disabled Living Foundation,
346 Kensington High Street,
London W4.

National Association for the Childless
318 Summer Lane,
Birmingham B19 3RL
021 359 4887

Health Education Council,
78 New Oxford Street,
London WC1.

IVF Counselling
Birmingham B19 3RL.
Tel. 021 359 4887/2113

Child,
367 Wandsworth Road,
London SW8.
Tel. 01 486 4289

Progress,
Campaigning for Research into Reproduction,
27–35 Mortimer Street,
London W1N 7RJ.
Tel. 01 580 9360

Miscarriage Association
18 Stoneybrook Close,
West Bretton,
Wakefield, West Yorkshire
WF4 4TP.
Tel. 092 485 515

Index

Note: Page numbering in bold type refers to illustrations